COLLINS GEM

MYTHOLOGY

C. M. Braysher

HarperCollins*Publishers*

C.M. Braysher has been a student of the folklore and mythology of different cultures for many years.

HarperCollins Publishers
Westerhill Road, Bishopbriggs, Glasgow G64 2QT

First published 2000

Reprint 10 9 8 7 6 5 4 3 2 1 0

Maps: Kevin Rhodie

Line illustrations: D. Braysher, K. Rhodie, J. Leo

ISBN 0 00 472370 8

Printed in Italy by Amadeus S.p.A.

CONTENTS

INTRODUCTION

Most of us think of ancient mythology as a set of tales of unfamiliar pagan gods and although this is true, it isn't the whole story. Ancient religions used stories and myths not just to express their religious beliefs but to describe their worlds and the powers that shaped them. So the ancient Egyptians, sun-baked, desert-bound and utterly dependent on the River Nile, had Ra, the Sun-god and Osiris, god of Vegetation and the flooding Nile as their foremost deities.

And myths didn't just express religious beliefs: historical myths were given a near-religious status in ancient Rome. Mythology can show much, not just about ancient worship but also about history, philosophy, science, morality and even climate.

As this book is meant primarily as an introduction to mythology I have chosen systems of beliefs that are either familiar in some ways, or are closest to home. So the Egyptians, Greeks and Romans, feeding off each other's influences, appear alongside the closer-to-home versions of the Celts and Norse. These tales, many of them thousands of years old, throw light not only on the cultures they come from but also on people's attitudes to the world – all giving their own fascinating angle on the constancy of human life and concerns.

EGYPTIAN MYTHOLOGY

Ancient Egypt

Ancient Egypt, with its characteristic pyramids and papyrus, sphinx and slaves, all-powerful pharaohs and their empire, hieroglyphics and mummies, delta floods and mysterious deities – was the first great nation of the Earth. It was dominant for a period of several thousand years before the birth of Christ, a pre-eminence it kept over several millenniums.

ORIGINS AND GROWTH

Although ancient Egypt had practically the same land area as modern-day Egypt does, it was originally two lands – Upper Egypt, the area inland around the Nile valley, and the more northern Lower Egypt that included the delta and coastal areas. The two were united under an Upper Egyptian king around 3100BC. The timeline of events on the following page shows Egypt's progression from then until the time of Christ.

THE KEY DATES IN EGYPT

c.3100 BC Upper and Lower Egypt united

c.3100-2649 BC The Archaic Period

c.2649-2134 BC The Old Kingdom One of Egypt's great periods. Government was strong, the country secure and wealthy, and writing, arts, sciences – including medicine and astronomy – all developed. It included the reign of Pepi II – at 94 years, the longest ever. This was also the age of the pyramids

c.2150-2040 BC The First Intermediate Period Egypt split in two once more

c.2040-1640 BC The Middle Kingdom Egypt reunited

c.1640-1552 BC The Second Intermediate Period The country split again

1552-1069 BC The New Kingdom Saw the empire expand under dynamic warrior pharaohs

1069-664 BC The Third Intermediate Period The country fell into decline

664-332 BC The Late Period Egypt regained some of its former greatness with relative peace and economic stability

332–30 BC Egypt conquered by Alexander the Great and ruled after his death by his general, Ptolemy, and his line. They in turn were conquered by the Romans; Cleopatra was the last of the line.

Egyptian Culture and its Mythology

CULTURAL INFLUENCES

Unlike other cultures, ancient Egypt grew in relative stability. With deserts and inhospitable lands on three sides and the Mediterranean to the north deterring any invasion, the civilisation developed with seemingly little outside influence, and used its own experiences to shape its mythology.

THE NILE

Most Egyptians were farmers who lived on the fertile lands bordering the length of the River Nile. The river and its movements were the single most important factor in their lives. As well as providing water for drinking, it nourished the land for crop-growing where there would otherwise have been only desert. As it flooded the plains each July, it fertilised the fields with its rich silt deposits before flowing away into the irrigation system built to channel it. The lush green fields at the Nile's edge also contrasted starkly with the barren and lifeless desert beyond, impressing forcefully on the Egyptians the closeness of the forces of life and death. Their mythology came to reflect the ancient Egyptians' total dependence on the Nile.

THE NATURAL WORLD

The other rhythmic patterns and forces of the natural world around them were strongly represented in the ancient Egyptians' religion. The greatest gods represented the great cosmic forces – most notably the life-giving sun – but there were also gods of the water, air and earth. Other gods, more local and more minor, looked after the human-sized concerns of everyday and family life – from patrons of farming, hunting and weaving to protectors of pregnant women, babies and children. And many gods were associated with certain animals or birds – the cat, the hawk, the fish and other creatures all became sacred in their own right. The snake was considered the most powerful creature, and came to represent the pharaoh himself. To make them easy to recognise, some gods were depicted with the head of their associated creature; for example Anubis, the god of the dead, always appeared with the head of a jackal.

DEATH

In common with most religions, the ancient Egyptians believed in an afterlife. Death was the stage everyone would pass through to the next life, which would be lived in a land to the far west – often called the Kingdom of the West. An elaborate set of burial rituals had to be observed, and there was a detailed account of the reception to be expected by the virtuous and by the sinful once they reached their final destination.

DEATH AND THE NEXT WORLD

BURIAL

Ironically, the ancient Egyptians' burial practices were what let us know so much about their lives. Their writings, inscribed on papyrus and carved on tombs, coffins and pyramids, give details of everyday life and its routines; the preserved and mummified corpses hold precious clues on everything from diet and health to hairdressing, make-up and fashions.

It was important that the dead person's body survived for the afterlife: the soul, the *ka*, needed to have its body intact, and different ways evolved to ensure this. The early pre-dynastic period saw bodies buried in shallow graves in the hot sand, where they dried out

Pyramids: important for survival in the next world

quickly and so were preserved. Chamber burials later became fashionable for the rich, but the bodies had to be embalmed to preserve them. By the time of the New Kingdom (1552–1069 BC) an elaborate set of rituals had grown up around the practice.

Embalming Bodies went to the embalmer's, the *wabet*. He opened the left side of the body to take out the internal organs; these were put in pillar-shaped canopic jars, often decorated with hieroglyphics and with the head of a sacred animal or deity. The body was dried out with salt, then stuffed with preservatives like resin, salt and special cloths to ready it for the next stage.

Mummifying Wrapping the corpse in linen bandages was not a casual exercise: it was done carefully and precisely, with magical words and charms said over each body part as it was wrapped; this guaranteed whole-body protection. Protective amulets like ankhs and scarabs were layered among the bandages, the mummy was perfumed and magical rites involving the laying on of precious stones followed.

Protective amulets like the djed (left), symbol of Osiris and of stability, and the ankh (right), representing life, banished evil

Finally, dressed in the ceremonial mask of Anubis, god of the dead and of embalmers, the embalmer finished by anointing and wrapping the head. The 36 separate substances used in the embalming process were put into the corpse's left hand – these represented the various forms of the god Osiris. The wrapping was completed, a prayer said and the body then went to its coffin.

Coffins The style of coffins changed over the centuries and millenniums. Earlier, Old Kingdom (2649–2134 BC) versions were plain or carried hieroglyphics, but by the time of the Middle Kingdom the more familiar Egyptian humanoid coffins were in fashion. By the later New Kingdom, this style had evolved to nests of human-shaped coffins, like Russian nesting dolls, with the body in the centre.

Funerals As now, family and friends attended. If the deceased was rich, professional mourners would be hired, priests would attend and the person's belongings would be brought to be put in the tomb (there was usually a place where food offerings could be left, too). Animals might be brought and, sometimes, servants were sealed in alive to serve their lord in the afterlife. Prayers were said before the coffin was lowered into its sarcophagus, the outer stone coffin. The belongings were left, the burial chamber sealed and the mourners came away. The deceased was well on the way to the Next World – the Kingdom of the West.

ENTRY TO THE NEXT WORLD

- The dead person needed a ferryman to row him or her across the River of Death to the far shore

- Helped by their amulets and the spells, prayers and advice in their *Book of the Dead*, the dead person had to pass the trials of the serpent-guarded Twelve Gates and cross the Lake of Fire

- Once these were passed, 42 Assessors read a list of the deceased's sins. The dead person made a declaration of purity and sinlessness (see p.13)

- Judgment followed in the Hall of Osiris. The deceased's heart was balanced on a set of scales against the Feather of Truth, symbol of Ma'at, goddess of justice and truth (see p. 36). A sinful life meant the scales were unbalanced and destruction followed. A good life was rewarded by balanced scales and the prize of everlasting life with the ancestors in the Next World.

THE NEXT WORLD

Tomb-robbers of more recent centuries almost always found, buried with the bodies they disturbed, funerary books written in hieroglyphics for the deceased, carved on the inside of coffins and tomb walls, painted on pyramids or rolled in papyrus. With prayers, hymns, formulas and instructions, they were a guide that showed what to do, say and expect in the afterlife.

Taken together they were called the Book of the Dead.

The confession stresses negatives rather than positives but still reflects how crucial were water, crops and land in this farming society; and it is interesting to see where it resembles other religions' guides to right living.

DECLARATION OF PURITY BEFORE THE 42 ASSESSORS

I have not committed sins against men
I have not opposed my family and kin
I have not acted falsely in the Seat of Truth
I have not known men who were of no account
I have not defrauded the poor man of his goods
I have not done what the gods abominate
I have not vilified a slave to his master
I have not inflicted pain
I have not caused anyone to go hungry
I have not made any man weep
I have not committed murder
I have not stolen fields
I have not added to the weights on the scales
I have not driven the cattle from their pastures
I have not caught fish with bait of the bodies of the same kind of fish
I have not stopped water when it should flow
I am pure, I am pure, I am pure

RELIGIOUS PRACTICE

LOCAL PRACTICE

With over 2000 gods and goddesses, it seemed there was a deity for every occasion, but a typical Egyptian would not have worshipped all these gods. Just as Egypt comprised two kingdoms and many districts, so different gods were worshipped in different areas. With the civilisation strung out along the long length of the Nile, what we think of as an ordered set of beliefs came together gradually out of a series of local religions. But the various localities always retained

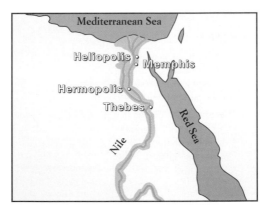

The four principal cult centres

their particular devotion to their own gods, and each cult centre thought of its god as the supreme one.

Cult Centres Some gods were only followed in their home areas and even the most important deities, like Ra, the sun god, who were worshipped across the

---

THE MAJOR CULT CENTRES

1 **Heliopolis** Ra or Atum was the supreme deity at Heliopolis, but eight other gods were also worshipped there: Geb, Isis, Nephthys, Nut, Osiris, Seth, Shu and Tefnut. The Greek-named city was near present-day Cairo in the Nile Delta.

2 **Memphis** The capital of Lower Egypt; home to the god Ptah, patron of the city; he was represented by the Apis Bull (*see p. 39*).

3 **Hermopolis** A group of eight gods was worshipped here, including Amon.

4 **Thebes (Luxor)** The capital of Upper Egypt. This was the latest of the major cult centres, rising to prominence in the XVII dynasty (c.1640–1552 BC), whose kings ruled from here. They established the Valley of the Kings and the Valley of the Queens burial grounds across the Nile from the city. Amon was their chief deity.

country, had a home town which was the centre of their cult and home to their main temple. The temple housed their main statue through which they communicated with the human world. The main cult centres were the rival bases of an array of the most important gods.

One Creation Myth All the cult centres shared a creation myth, believing that creation was a gradual process that the gods only intervened in on one occasion – The First Time. They disagreed mainly in the degree of importance they gave to their own group of deities, with some also expressing minor differences in the creation story. For example, at Heliopolis the god Atum, identified with Ra, appeared from the primeval waters on an island. But in other stories he was hatched from an egg, emerged from a lotus that grew in the mud, and appeared as a scarab beetle on the eastern horizon. The table on p. 17 shows the primordial creator gods that appeared in one of the most widely accepted of the creation myths.

THE PEOPLE

The temples were not like modern places of worship: Egyptian worshippers asking questions or seeking explanations would come to the temple gates with offerings, and scribes were there to copy down their questions and requests to pass to the temple priests. The public were rarely allowed inside, and the priests interpreted the god's response which came through an

THE OGDOAD (EIGHT DEITIES) OF HERMOPOLIS

These were the primordial gods of creation

Nun & Naunet	God and goddess of the primordial ocean or water abyss
Huh & Hauhet	God and goddess of eternity or infinite space
Kuk & Kauket	God and goddess of darkness
Amun & Amaunet	God and goddess of air

oracle – a message direct from the deity, by means of its cult statue. On feast days the cult statue was carried out of its temple on a sacred barque, or boat; then anyone could approach it with a question. The barque's subsequent movement indicated whether the god's reply was yes or no.

The gods were consulted over other matters, too: if a verdict couldn't be agreed in a trial, judges could ask the oracle. Several gods – such as Isis, Thoth, Sekhmet and Imhotep – were associated with healing, and their help was sought at times of illness. A patient could stay overnight in a special temple room in the hope of receiving a miraculous cure or dreaming of a cure.

Dreams were one way that the gods communicated with the people. Some priests were specially skilled in dream interpretation, and whole books were devoted to the subject. The gods also sent other signs: omens were read into unusual weather or movements in the skies. Pharaoh Tuthmosis III, who took Egypt's power to its zenith, was reassured by the sight of a shooting star in the night sky on the eve of a crucial battle.

THE KING

The Egyptian king claimed descent from the gods through the god Ra, said to have been the first king of Egypt. He was the intermediary between the people and the deities, and was the head of their cults. People prayed to statues of the king in the hope he could influence the gods on their behalf, and it was thought that the spirit of the god Horus came into him as he sat on his throne in royal regalia. The king was almost too godly to be called by name, so he was referred to by the word 'palace' – in Egyptian, *pero* – source of the term 'pharaoh'.

ANIMALS

It wasn't just the king who was thought sacred. Association with some gods and goddesses meant divine status was conferred on particular animals, and a life of pampered security was guaranteed for the lucky beast chosen to live at the temple and receive the god's spirit. These were some of the chosen animals at certain temples:

- Apis bull at Ptah's temple, Memphis
- a cat at Bast's temple in Bubastis
- a ram at Amun's temple at Karnak
- a hawk at Horus's temple at Edfu

The sacred status of these godly animals gradually spread to benefit other lucky pets. Into the last millennium BC, whole groups of species were being honoured in the hope of pleasing the gods. Dead pets might be buried with full mourning and honours; like their wealthy owners, they could be mummified and laid to rest in pet cemeteries, where their favourite toys were left with them. The Egyptians' fondness for keeping animal companions is testified to in the millions of animal remains that have been found.

The Gods of Egypt

As the series of local religions grew together over centuries and millenniums, Egypt's myth and religious practice continually evolved and changed against the background of shifting political and economic fortunes. This could mean, for example, that different gods were more revered at different times – although some stayed constant in people's affection. It also meant that, with few written records to draw on, the mythologies of individual gods overlapped, and some, like Horus, took on multiple personalities and different names for each of their manifestations or aspects.

RA

Of the many different versions of the sun god, Ra or Re is the commonest and most familiar to us. He took on many of the characteristics of Atum, an earlier sun-god worshipped at Heliopolis. Risen out of the vast waste of waters called Nun, Ra was represented by the sun at its fullest strength. As Zeus became greater than

The sacred eye of Ra, destroyer of his enemies

his father, Cronus, likewise Ra superseded Nun. He was believed to sail across the sky in a boat each day and through the Underworld at night.

Ra's family included some of the most important gods (*below*). He produced his own children, spitting out

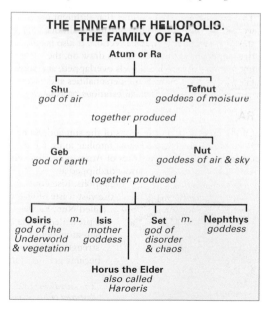

THE ENNEAD OF HELIOPOLIS.
THE FAMILY OF RA

Atum or Ra

Shu
god of air

Tefnut
goddess of moisture

together produced

Geb
god of earth

Nut
goddess of air & sky

together produced

Osiris   *m.*   **Isis**
*god of the   mother
Underworld   goddess
& vegetation*

Set   *m.*   **Nephthys**
*god of   goddess
disorder
& chaos*

Horus the Elder
*also called
Haroeris*

Shu, god of air, and vomiting up Tefnut, goddess of rain.

Ra's cult hit its peak in the Old Kingdom, and his cult was adopted officially by the pharaohs who called themselves 'sons of Ra'. This was also the age of the pyramids, and pharaohs from the 4th Dynasty on (c.2575–2467 BC), which included King Cheops, were buried in pyramids. Scholars have speculated on the significance of the pyramid, with some claiming they was a means for the dead pharaoh, entombed within, to climb in the afterlife to his father Ra in the heavens. And the sun's rays are recalled in the pyramid's shape. However, this system only allowed afterlife places for the king and the favoured relatives and courtiers buried near him.

The falcon-headed Ra or Horus, wearing the crowns of Upper and Lower Egypt

The worship of Ra, and the other forms of the sun god, was never embraced by everyone. The remoteness and untouchability of both the sun and the pharaoh, its human personification, meant that sun worship stayed essentially a royal and a state religion. Ordinary people had other gods closer to their hearts.

OSIRIS

In the centuries between the time of the Old and Middle Kingdoms (c.2150–2040 BC), Egyptian religion went through a gradual but fundamental change in emphasis, mirroring the breakdown

Osiris – ruler of the dead, god of the Underworld, of vegetation and the Nile. Symbol of the triumph of good over evil and of the hope of salvation for all Egyptians

of the absolute power of the pharaohs. As royal power and status crumbled, so by the time of the Middle Kingdom tombs were built by anyone who could afford them and a cult came to flourish that emphasised universal salvation and a place in the afterlife for all, royal or not.

HIS STORY

The Osiris myth related his own triumph over death and the roots of the hope of resurrection for all, that he was able to offer.

Although the son of Geb and Nut (see p. 21), Osiris ruled in Egypt as a human god, bringing stability, wealth and order in a barbarous land. But he unwittingly aroused the murderous hatred and jealousy of his brother, Set. Set had made a wooden chest, built exactly to fit his brother's dimensions, and lured him into it, only to close it up and seal it shut.

Set: often depicted with the head of a dog, he was god of chaos and disorder

The chest was thrown into the sea at the mouth of the Nile. It was ultimately recovered by Isis, Osiris's wife, but Set discovered the body and chopped his brother's remains into pieces, scattering them across Egypt. Isis, helped by Nephthys and Anubis, faithfully recovered all the pieces of her husband's body and, using her own powers and healing skills, reconstituted him and brought him to life again.

When Horus, the son of Osiris and Isis, became ruler in Egypt, his father went to rule the Kingdom of the Dead, sitting in judgement on every soul who entered.

HIS ROLES

Osiris was the god of vegetation, especially corn and trees, and also of the flooding Nile – roles that emphasised his place in the annual cycle of death and rebirth that took place on the land in this life. His other role was as god of the dead and judge in the Underworld.

HIS POPULARITY

As the pharaohs' total power and the cult of Ra waned, so Osiris's grew, especially during the time of the Middle Kingdom. Even after the return of strong royal government in Egypt, Osiris never lost his appeal. In his life and death story he promised rebirth, resurrection and a place in the afterlife to all, regardless of status. His temples were found throughout the kingdom and his holy day was celebrated annually at the year's end. In his death and return he personified the annual drought and the return of the Nile floods to the land, and his victory over his wicked brother promised the ultimate triumph of Good over Evil.

THE OTHER GODS

Osiris and Ra are still two of the best known of the Egyptian gods, but there were countless others. What follows is a listing of some of the best-known ones.

Amon, Amun, Amon-Ra (The Invisible One) Worshipped first at Thebes where he was seen as a creator-god, Amon's cult later grew to national prominence under the Thebes-originated 18th Dynasty of the New Kingdom. During this time he was associated with the sun-god, Ra (*see p. 20*), as Amon-Ra, and was called King of the Gods. *Associated animals:* ram, goose

Anubis (God of the Dead and of Embalmers) The jackal-headed son of Osiris and Nephthys, conceived after his mother tricked Osiris into sleeping with her. He was abandoned by his mother and brought up by Isis, later helping her embalm and preserve Osiris's dismembered body.

Despite his fearsome associations with a scavenger, Anubis was seen as a protector of the bodies of the dead, both from jackals and from decay. Chief embalmers wore ceremonial Anubis-masks in acknowledgement of their patron. He was also a

Anubis, jackal-headed god of the dead

compassionate but fair overseer at Judgement Day, weighing the heart of the deceased in the scales against the feather of truth. *Associated animals:* jackal, dog

Apis Bull See *p. 40.*

Aten (The Sun) Actually the sun-disk. The sun had various divine manifestations (*see p. 34*). Worship of Aten was part of the pattern of a royal sun-worship cult and was never fully embraced by ordinary people. King Akhenaten of the 18th Dynasty became the first known person in history to worship only one god when he tried – without any lasting success – to make Aten-worship the only official religion, banning the worship of other gods. (Incidentally, Akhenaten's family were to become more famous than he was: his wife was Queen Nefertiti (*see p. 28*) and Tutankhamun was his son.)

Atum (The Whole, Complete) The original

Akhenaten's queen, Nefertiti

primordial creator-god whose cult centre was at Heliopolis (*see p. 15*). By the time of the Old Kingdom, when the pharaohs' worship of Ra was at its height, Atum's cult and features had been subsumed into Ra's.

Bast, Bastet, Pasht (Goddess of Bubastis) Bast was a protective mother-goddess, caring for pregnant women, and protecting men against disease. She was patroness of cats, and was also goddess of music, dance and joy. She represented the healing power of the sun.

This mother-goddess's popularity grew in the Late Period, even spilling over Egypt's boundaries into other lands. Hugely popular festivals were held in her honour at her

city, Bubastis, in the Delta region. Any cat that died
during the year was embalmed and brought here to be
buried. Festive celebrations lasted several days and
nights, with hundreds of thousands of high-spirited
revellers reputedly drinking more wine in one week
than in the rest of the year put together.
Associated animal: cat

Bes (God of Childbirth, Art and Music) Despite his
grotesque appearance, this scary-looking little dwarf-
god was one of the most popular in the Egyptian
pantheon. A jester-god who was a protector of
pregnant women, those in labour and of children, his
image was usually hung around the household as an
amulet to ward off evil. He was also one of the gods
worshipped in the home. But Bes had alternative,
darker side to his personality: as a warrior-god, he
ripped out the hearts of the wicked and unworthy in
death, while still remaining a friend to the righteous
and the good.

Geb (God of the Earth) One of the primordial gods
of Heliopolis, Geb was the partner of Nut, his sister,
goddess of the sky: this is how they are depicted
symbolically (*see p. 30*). The pair were forcibly
separated and the resulting tears Geb cried were
enough to fill the rivers, seas and oceans of the earth.
Their children were Set, Nephthys, Isis and Osiris.

Geb was known as the Great Cackler – a reference to

*Earth god and Sky goddess, Geb and Nut; Shu, god of the air,
supports her*

a popular creation myth in which Geb, as a goose, had
laid the egg from which the world came. He is often
depicted with a goose on his head.

Associated animal: goose

Hapi (God of the Nile) Appearing as a man with a
woman's breasts, Hapi was one of the highest-ranking
gods, with both strength and nurturing qualities. He
could also be destructive, representing the Nile's heavy
floods. His status ranked alongside the creator-gods,
and he later became identified with Osiris – also god
of the Nile. Hapi united the country, and was depicted
crowned with papyrus plants for the northern Nile
and lotus plants for the south.

Haroeris See *Horus*.

Hathor (Goddess of Joy, Love and Beauty) The mother, wife and daughter of Horus was shown at times with the head of a cow and later wearing a cow's horns. Various scholars have tried to explain her all-encompassing relationship with Horus – such as with Hathor as a moon goddess, giving birth to, appearing with, and coming after, Horus as the sun.

Worship of Hathor was Egypt-wide but her main temple was in Denderah which also played host to the annual drunken orgy that was her birthday celebration. This feast recalled a legend of Hathor and Horus: Horus, growing old, found himself mocked and about to be replaced by his worshippers. In fury, he send Hathor to punish them but she went too far, glorying in the slaughter. Horus had to intervene again, this time to save humanity from Hathor's bloodlust. He sent a flood of beer to earth to make her drunk and so stop the killing. The beer in the story paralleled

Hathor, depicted in the form of a cow

the Nile's inundation, and Hathor's festival was celebrated in Thoth, the first month of the flood.

Although a goddess of death, Hathor's other forms were more benign. She was goddess of the west where the afterworld was and was said to nourish the dead in the afterlife. She came to newborn children to tell their fate, appearing as seven young women – the Seven Hathors. She embodied the attractive elements of femininity and ultimately the Egyptians thought all goddesses were represented in her.

Associated animal: cow

Horus, Haroeris, Her, Heru One of the most important figures in the Egyptian pantheon, the first Horus was one of the gods of Heliopolis, son of Geb and Nut and brother of Osiris, Isis, Set and Nephthys; he came to be identified with the ruling pharaoh. Known as Horus the elder, he fought, in the form of a sun-disk with outstretched wings, on behalf of his father, Ra, against his wicked brother Set, always defeating but never completely eradicating him. The good (represented by the light of the sun-disk) would always triumph over the dark Set, symbolising evil.

Horus was a sky-god, represented as the figure of a man with a hawk's head, and also with the moon in his left eye and the sun in his right. In one version of the Horus myth, he lost his left eye in battle with Set who was later forced by Ra, his father, to restore it. The loss of Horus's moon-eye explained the moon's various phases throughout the month. In the other main version of his myth, Horus was also related to Osiris, but this time as his son. He was conceived after Set killed his father, and, after Osiris's resurrection, father and son ultimately ensured the triumph of good over evil by vanquishing the wicked Set. Horus the Child became the living pharaoh of Egypt, and the god was often depicted wearing the red and white crown of a united Egypt, while his father, Osiris, became ruler of the Underworld, identified with the dead pharaoh. Horus the Child was also one of Egypt's most popular gods, and images of him seated as an infant on his mother's knee are compared to Virgin and Child iconography.

Temple of Isis

These two were were not the only forms but the various other Horus derivatives in the pantheon of Egyptian gods all derived from aspects of the original. *Associated animal:* hawk or falcon

Isis (Goddess of Corn, of Crafts and of Fertility) A child of Ra, chief goddess and queen of the gods. As explained in Osiris's story (*see p. 23*), Isis set out on a long quest to find the lost body of her brother-husband, murdered by Set. Her devotion and skill with help from the god Thoth ultimately helped bring him back from the dead and she conceived Horus (*see p. 32*) by him. Her son, too, was killed by Set, this time in the form of a scorpion until Thoth came to her aid again.

Isis's sufferings on her quest and her love that endured beyond death won her great affection in the hearts of all followers. As one of the most beloved

ASPECTS OF THE SUN

The sun was worshipped in its various phases

Khepri	The rising sun with a scarab beetle (*see p. 35*)
Ra	The sun at its midday strength (*see p. 20*)
Atum	The sun setting as an old man (*see p. 28*)
Aten	The sun-disk

deities, her cult spread into other areas: the Greeks worshipped her, as did the Romans right up to the 5th century AD; even today remnants of Isis-worship still exist in Egypt.

Khepri, Khepera (The Rising Sun) Khepri appeared on the eastern horizon as a scarab beetle, pushing the new sun ahead of him in the sky as a beetle would push its egg across the desert sands. He was a creator-god and was one of the aspects of the sun-god Ra, or Atum, head of the nine gods worshipped at the cult centre at Heliopolis. The table on page 34 shows some of the aspects the same god could take on.

Associated animal: scarab beetle

Khunum (The Potter Creator-God) Originally a god of Upper Egypt where he was thought to control the source of the Nile, Khunum's cult centre

The scarab beetle, sacred to the sun gods and a symbol of rebirth in the afterlife

Ram-headed Khunum,
the potter-god

was at Elephantine where the Nile's source was thought to be. He was also depicted as a potter who moulded people on his wheel, with two figures under his hands – the person's *ba* and *ka*: the body and inner person. *Associated animal:* ram

Khonsu, Khons (Moon God, Expeller of Devils) This god with healing powers was the son of Amun and Mut; all were worshipped at their Karnak cult centre.

Ma'at, Ma (Goddess of Truth and Justice) Ma'at, wife of Thoth, personified the balance of the universe. Her priests were sometimes taken from the ranks of judges, and she was depicted standing behind the pharaoh, head of the earthly legal system. She was such a powerful symbol of justice that she was

thought present at the declaration before the 42 Assessors in the Underworld, when the dead person recited the Confession of Purity (*see p. 13*). Passing from there to the Hall of Osiris, the deceased declared that he or she had 'done Ma'at' before Anubis weighed their heart in the judgement scales against the feather of truth.
Associated icon: ostrich feather

Min (God of Fertility, Crops and the Harvest) As well as emphasising his place as a god of sexual potency, Min was a god of travellers. He was sometimes identified with Horus.
Associated animal: bull

Neith (Goddess of Crafts and Wisdom) Sais was the home of Neith's cult and when the 26th Dynasty made the city the capital, Neith-worship became more prominent. She wore the red crown of Lower Egypt but as a craft goddess she was also said to have woven the world on her loom.

Nephthys (Goddess of Death and Magic) As the sister of Osiris, Isis and Horus, sister-wife of Set, daughter of Nut and Geb, and mother of Anubis, she played a part in one of the most important Egyptian myths (*see p. 25*). Although she was one of the gods from the cult centre of Heliopolis, Nephthys was noted more for her relations with the other gods than in her own right. She represented the shadow of what Isis stood for: decay, death and a wasting away; although in other aspects her role as a goddess of regeneration is also important.

Nu, Nun (God of the Primordial Ocean) First and oldest of the gods, according to some myths, from whom all life sprang. Hermopolis was his cult centre.

Nut (Goddess of the Sky) One of Heliopolis's original creator-gods. In the most common version of her myth she is shown with her brother-partner, Geb, the earth god (*see p. 30*), towering over the earth, touching beyond it with her toes and fingers, her body's arch shape representing the sky. She was the personification of the sky and of the morning. She and Geb had five children: Osiris, Horus, Isis, Nephthys and Set.

Nut also played a part in the rituals of the dead: her image was painted on coffins, she was mentioned in the Book of the Dead and was believed to refresh the deceased every day, letting them shelter in the branches of her sacred tree, the sycamore.

Osiris See *p. 23*.

Ptah (Creator-God of Memphis) The supreme, creator-god of Memphis, closely connected with the Apis Bull (*see below*). The cult followers at Memphis claimed that Atum, foremost of the gods of Heliopolis, was Ptah's son, so staking out a claim for the superiority and antiquity of their own cult. Ptah was a god of crafts, the patron of artisans, and the architect of the universe and creator of everything in it. Another myth had him creating as a metalworker.

Ra, Re, Phra See *p. 20.*

Renenutet (Goddess of the Harvest) This goddess was the partner of Sebek, the god of water. Her temple at Fayum was one of the minor cult centres. *Associated animal:* snake

Sakhmet, Sekhmet (Mother goddess of Memphis) The lion-headed wife of Ptah was associated particularly with healing and medicine. Her name also meant

---

THE APIS BULL

- Connected with the god Ptah – his spirit entered it at special holy festivals

- The bull's dung, and his mother's milk, were used in medicine and healing

- When the sacred bull died he was called the Osiris-Apis and buried with honours in a special tomb at Sakkara.

- Egypt was searched to find a successor, always known by certain characteristics: black-and-white colouring, a scarab-shaped lump on his tongue, a white triangle on his face, a vulture-shaped marking on his back and double tail-hairs.

'powerful', and she was worshipped as a war-goddess. And unlike the more famous cat-goddess Bast, Sakhmet represented the sun's destructive rather than healing power, and the fieriness of the desert. *Associated animal:* lioness

Sebek, Sobek (The God of Water) Egyptians had a relationship with the crocodile which was at best ambivalent, an attitude echoed in the reverence and revulsion this god was held in. On the one hand the country lived in fear of crocodiles in the times of drought when they left the river-bed to look for food, and crocodile-hunting was a popular upper-class sport. On the other, they were also seen as national guardians, deterring invasion from neighbouring lands.

In mythology, Sebek was a helper of Isis and Osiris, but was also identified with their evil brother, Set. And some accounts of

Crocodile god Sebek

the afterworld stated that Sebek helped to guide the
newly-dead to safety through the numerous dangers of
the Underworld. The harvest-goddess Renenutet was
his wife and both were venerated at El Faiyum.
Associated animal: crocodile

Set, Seth (God of the Desert, Darkness, Trouble and,
later, Evil) The story of Set has been part-recounted
in the myths of his enemies: Osiris (*see p. 24*), his
brother and Horus the Child (*see p. 33*), his nephew.

Set's ultimate identification with evil was not how his
cult started out. He was a god of the night sky, storms
and earthquakes, and of the north, a place associated
with death – all undesirable but inevitable, and none
of them evil. In one incarnation he was a friend of the
dead and of Osiris. He was worshipped in Upper Egypt
and his cult also held sway in the Delta. His birthday
was celebrated at the year's end with those of his siblings. The decline in Set worship is usually explained
in political terms: for example, one theory argues that
it began after the invasion of the Hyksos, who became
rulers in the 15th and 16th Dynasties. The Hyksos
worshipped Set, so the native Egyptians distanced
themselves from him. Another explanation states that
in the constant rivalries between the priesthoods of
various gods, Set's priests lost out to those of Horus.

Set was portrayed as a man with the head of an
indeterminate animal which has been seen as many

creatures, from an aardvark to a dog. Others have seen the horn-like ears as a forerunner of depictions of the horned Satan in Christianity. Set himself was supposed to have had a shock of red hair – perhaps the reason for the prejudice against red-heads that still exists, or just another example of the age-old practice. Egyptians with red colouring were badly treated, although not as badly as some russet-coated animals: the writer Plutarch noted the ass was despised in many areas, and killed in some, because its coat was reddish in colour.

Associated animals: black boar, donkey, hippopotamus

Shu (God of the Air and Atmosphere) Another of the original Heliopolis gods, Shu was the son of Atum, later Ra, partner of Tefnut and father of Nut, the sky goddess and Geb, the earth god. In the normal depiction of Geb and Nut (*see p. 30*), Shu is often shown between the two, holding up his daughter above the earth; he is responsible for separating earth and sky.

Tawaret, Tauert (Goddess of Birth) A grotesque hippopotamus goddess who, like her equally ugly husband Bes, had no temple but was one of the most popular and revered gods in the whole Egyptian pantheon. Pregnant women and those in childbirth revered her, entrusting to her their own safety and that of their child. She was said to have been the nurse of the gods.

Tefnut (Goddess of Moisture and Rain) Partner of Shu, the sky god, Tefnut was the daughter of Atum or Ra and one of the nine creator-gods worshipped at Heliopolis.

Thoth (God of the Moon, Wisdom, Learning, Speech and Time, inventor of writing and scribe to the gods) As well as this lengthy list of skills and attributes,

Thoth was a magician and ruled the Underworld. Other gods turned to him in time of trouble, and he helped the dead through the perilous processes leading to judgement, too – he was the recorder of souls who delivered the final judgement and was said to have written the *Book of the Dead*. He could grant longer life if he wished – he restored Isis to life in one story, after Horus had cut off her head in anger, and he judged the battle between Horus and Set.

Usually depicted writing: Thoth

He was closely connected with Ra – according to some, his myth was derived from Ra's – and was the moon god to Ra's sun. His cult centre was Hermopolis. Thoth is normally depicted ibis-headed: the bird was sacred to him, and worshippers offered it in sacrifice to him.

Associated animals: ibis, baboon

Divine figures on a painted papyrus

GREEK MYTHOLOGY

Ancient Greece

At the same time as ancient Egypt was flourishing, there was beginning another formative and influential civilisation on another Mediterranean shore. Ancient Greece, first under the Minoans on Crete then under the Mycenaeans in their mainland kingdoms, was growing in power through the eras of the Old and New kingdoms in Egypt. But the time that we generally think of as being 'ancient Greece', with Homer and Socrates, the first Olympic Games and the Spartan Wars, slavery, democracy and trial by jury, was in the final century BC.

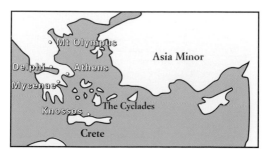

THE KEY DATES IN GREECE

c.6500–2900 BC The Neolithic Period
The first settlers arrived on Crete
Pottery made on Crete and the Greek mainland
Metal-working began; evidence on the Cyclades

c.2900–1000 BC The Bronze Age
Craft- and metal-working widespread
Troy founded, c.2500 BC
Sailing ships used on the Aegean, c.2000 BC
Minoans flourishing on Crete, c.1900 BC
Mycenaeans flourishing on mainland, c.1600 BC
Trojan War began, c.1250 BC

c.1100–800 BC The Dark Ages
Mycenaean civilisation broke down

c.800–500 BC The Archaic Period
Homer lived
The first Olympic Games were held, c.776 BC
Tyrants seized power in Greek mainland states
The Persian Wars began

c.500–336 BC The Classical Age
Democracy replaced the tyrants
Spartan Wars with other states
Philip of Macedonia became ruler of Greece,
337 BC; succeeded by his son Alexander who
conquered all neighbouring lands; he died 323 BC

c.323–30 BC The Hellenistic Period
Continuing wars among the Greek states
resulted in defeat and control by Rome

Greek Culture and its Mythology

Greece was not as fortunate as Egypt when it came to freedom from outside influences. Throughout its history, culture and civilisation had developed and grown against constant insecurities and aggressions, both within its own states and from outside, that threatened at times to become overwhelming – as happened in the Dark Ages. What has survived of Greek art and literature shows many different influences, so much so that no one has yet come up with a single, all-encompassing explanation of the mythology.

The disruptions in Greece's development meant fewer ancient artefacts survived than in Egypt. Burial practices and climate also played a part – whereas Egypt's underground tombs and hot

Homer: an important source in Greek myth

desert sands preserved its archaeological evidence, in Greece little has remained to offer clues to historians.

In fact there were relatively few clues to Greek belief

GREEK MYTHOLOGY: THE IMPORTANT EARLY WRITERS

Homer (lived 8thC BC) Presumed author of the oldest stories of Greek mythology, the *Iliad* and the *Odyssey*. He was said to be blind and to have lived in Ionia but hardly anything else is known of him.

The *Homeric Hymns* in praise of various gods like Apollo, were also once thought to have been his work. These were the main sources of the myths about several of the most important gods.

Hesiod (lived late 8thC BC) From poor and obscure farming origins, Hesiod is the supposed author of *Theogony*, relating the gods' beginnings and the battles between the Olympians and Titans.

Pindar (born c.520 BC) A poet who composed odes in honour of the winners at various games, such as the Olympics. He often used mythology in his work and is one of the most important early sources.

Aeschylus (525–426 BC), **Sophocles** (497–405 BC), **Euripides** (485–407 BC) Playwrights whose surviving tragedies often feature characters from myth.

and mythology. One of the most important was the pottery and ceramics of the time (*see for example p. 120*) – much of it featuring painted scenes from everyday life, but also popular were depictions of the gods and stories from mythology, often different from the surviving stories told by the important Greek writers.

CULTURAL INFLUENCES

The Greek people were made up of a continuous stream of incoming tribes, each bringing its own heroes and mythology. Legend overlaid history and traditional story in the retelling but each new addition was an add on, never a replacement, with the result that a hugely elaborate set of myths evolved. And myth was treated like history: Heracles was the legendary hero of the Spartans, and even in battle negotiations, mythical events were used as bargaining chips, having the apparent status of recent history. This blending of myth with reality was not just the habit of people with an oral-history tradition – myth was part of everyday reality, from the local cult to the great pantheon of gods on Olympus. The places that the gods had visited were carefully recorded, and many families even claimed divine ancestry, so close were inter-relations between humans and deities. The philosopher Plato was said to be descended from Poseidon through both his parents, Alexander the Great claimed descent from Heracles, and ordinary people expected divine visitation into their lives on a daily basis.

Greek mythology was an attempt to explain the harshness and the mysteries of life, from sickness and normal, everyday hardships, to sacrifice and the mysteries of elements like fire or the weather.

THE NATURAL WORLD

The supernatural beliefs of the geographically self-contained Egyptians could be explained almost wholly in relation to the world around them; but for the Greeks, their landscape was simply the backdrop to the divine dramas the gods played out.

And their world was not as predictable year by year as their neighbours' to the south: for example, the 2nd century BC Minoan civilisation on Crete is now thought to have been shattered by a massive volcanic eruption on the island of Thera (now Santorini). Half of Thera was blasted away by the force of the explosion which caused tremors and brought tsunamis to Crete 70 miles away, wrecking buildings and destroying crops.

Earthquakes also had a part to play. The eastern

Mediterranean is an earthquake hot-spot, and while houses and communities could be rebuilt after a tremor hit, the effect of an unpredictable world on the psyche may well have contributed to the notion of a set of capricious and petulant gods.

INSTABILITY AND STRIFE

Homer's works made the Trojan War the most famous Greek conflict, but the possibility of strife was an ever-present fact of life in this part of the world, right up to the time of Alexander the Great and Greece's eventual conquest by Rome. The male citizens of one Greek state, Sparta, even lived permanently in barracks, training and practising under the harshest conditions so they would be constantly prepared for war. Whole towns were known to have been displaced by tyrants in warfare, with many of their inhabitants choosing to kill themselves and their families rather than leave them to the cruelties of the victors. This constant threat of war with other Greek states or with outsiders saw heavily fortified city-states evolve.

But the Greeks had to contend with more than just a threat of external strife. Within their settlements, conflict was a part of everyday life. Heroic and noble ambition were the ideals, but the reality was quite different. Envy and revenge were positively encouraged, mockery and ridicule, especially of public figures, was the norm (ultimately driving many, such as Poliagros, to suicide) and happiness, being transitory, was discouraged. Pain was declared the only certainty before death. A detached attitude to death was felt the best one to cultivate; there would then be less sorrow at parting, and life's inevitable disappointments would be avoided. Such a constant emphasis on insecurity and conflict had its effect on the Greeks' worldview and the development of their mythology with its strong emphasis on fate, misfortune and tragedy.

DEATH

Death was the means of entering the Underworld, ultimate resting-place of the souls of the dead. The proper conduct of the death rites was essential if the deceased had a hope of being able to cross into Hades.

DEATH AND THE NEXT WORLD

BURIAL

Funeral rites were essential if the soul of a dead person was to be allowed into the Underworld: the unfortunates who didn't receive this respect were doomed to wander forever on the banks of the River Styx, in a limbo among neither living nor dead. Some people even had children primarily so there would be someone to carry out the rites at their own funeral.

Funerals A coin was left in the corpse's mouth as the fare to pay Charon, ferryman of dead souls across the Styx. The body was dressed for the funeral and left in state so visitors could come to pay their respects.

OEDIPUS – A GREEK TRAGEDY

One of the most famous characters in Greek tragedy was Oedipus, the man fated to kill his father and marry his mother. Although his royal parents tried to avert the foretold disaster by exposing him at birth, he was saved and brought up by adoptive parents.

In later life he was involved in a quarrel over rights of way on the road and in a fit of rage killed his opponent – unknown to him, his birth father, Laïus, King of Thebes. Oedipus went on to kill the Sphinx that threatened to destroy Thebes and so won the hand of the widowed queen Jocasta – his birth mother.

A plague in the city after years of Oedipus's rule prompted a delegation to Delphi, where the Oracle advised the reason for the city's misfortune. As realisation dawned with the tale's unravelling, Jocasta hanged herself and Oedipus poked his own eyes out. He ended his life in exile, cursing his sons who did nothing to save him from banishment.

Women of the family would cut their hair short and family and friends wore black to show they were in mourning. On the funeral day the corpse was laid on a cart or bier, still open to view, and taken to the cemetery accompanied by mourners – professionals hired specially for the occasion, if the family could afford it.

Burial Each family had its own plot and fashions here changed – cremation was popular in the Dark Ages, but burial came back in the last millennium BC. Tombs were marked with anything from a marble slab to a stone sarcophagus or even a mock-temple construction for the well-to-do. The ashes of the cremated were buried in jars in the grave. Like the Egyptians, personal belongings for use in the afterlife were left with the corpse and family members continued to bring offerings, such as perfume, for the dead.

THE NEXT WORLD

Hermes (*see p. 92*) took to the entrance to Hades the dead person's soul or shade – the bodyless, conscious-ness-less shadow of their living self. Many believed Hades was under the earth, others thought it was in western Greece or even Italy. Wherever it was, it was never believed to be the place of unspeakable torment and damnation that emerged in the Christian model.

But entry was not automatic – without the proper funeral rites or fare to pay the ferryman, the shade would be doomed to wander forever in limbo on the banks of the Styx, boundary of Hades and boundary between the worlds of the living and the dead.

Charon ferried the dead across the Styx where they passed Cerberus, three-headed dog guardian of the gateway to the Underworld. No living soul could get into Hades past him, and no dead souls out.

SISYPHUS

One of Hades's most famous inmates was Sisyphus, the wily King of Ephyra. He had involved himself in various family quarrels while alive. Sisyphus acted so badly in one unspecified quarrel that he was condemned to eternal punishment – pushing a boulder uphill, only to have it roll back down to the bottom each time it approached the top.

Judgement Judgement by the gatekeepers, or judges, Aeacus, Minos and his brother Rhadamanthys, followed. But their duties must have been limited, as any shades who had been sentenced to eternal damnation in Tartarus had already been sent there by the gods, in any case. The Erinyes, hideously ugly female spirits, were thought to torture the damned in Hades. A few others, beloved of the gods, lived not as shades but in full ownership of their faculties, in Elysium.

But for most souls, whose relatively unremarkable lives consigned them to neither extreme, the Plain of Asphodel became their home. After drinking from the Pool of Lethe they lost all memory of their former selves and spent countless colourless days wandering aimlessly, sometimes replaying scenes from their past life, now without pain or pleasure.

RELIGIOUS PRACTICE

THE GODS – ALL TOO HUMAN

The Greeks' gods seem unusual to modern eyes. In the things they did and in their motives, they were too close to humans to be thought sacred or divine. The only moral examples they set were bad ones – abuse of power, domination, pleasure-seeking, vengeance and boundless egotism were all the godly characteristics. They were not even all-powerful: they had to share power with the Fates – up to three remote beings who governed particularly the start and the end of human life – and so had only limited control of events. And they suffered so much from human failings that they were unhappy. Human life was bound often to be wretched and miserable, and the gods ensured everyone received their full portion. Fate and the jealousy of the gods determined the destiny even of heroes, regardless of their moral righteousness. Consequently, instead of being revered, they were feared.

THE PEOPLE

No one was instructed in religion and although worship was not compulsory, most people practised it. Those especially devoted to a particular deity could delve deeper through initiation into the god's dedicated and usually secret cult; they were promised the ultimate reward of an afterlife in the Elysian Fields. But for most people, normal forms of worship were enough.

Worship Worship did not take place in temples, but often in homes where prayers could be said and an offering made – usually of wine, called a libation – at a small altar. People would remember the gods as they went about their daily business – for example, someone setting out on a hunt might pray for success to Artemis, the goddess who governed hunting. For a particular request, a worshipper would take an offering in sacrifice to the god's temple.

Temples The gods each had their own temples and priests or priestesses who made sure that the rules of offering and worship were followed. The closeness of godly–human contact meant the temple was seen as the god's home on earth, and temple designs were based on palaces. Inside the temple, in a room called the *cella*, stood the cult statue of the god to whom the temple was dedicated; the statue of Zeus in his temple at Olympia was over 43 ft (13 m) high, was made of gold and ivory and was one of the seven wonders of the ancient world. An altar stood, usually at the temple entrance, where worshippers could bring food or drink, animals or birds for sacrifice by the priest, according to normally strict rules. But for major undertakings, people tried various ways to discover the gods' will.

Foretelling the Future Direct communication with a deity was possible through an oracle. In one of these revered places, a special priest or priestess would pass on the message of a god in answer to a question. The most famous of the Greek oracles was Apollo's temple at Delphi, where his priestess, the Pythia, conveyed his replies to particular questions. Such was the popularity of the Pythia's consultations that their frequency increased from annually to weekly, and she had to recruit another Pythia. The priestess bathed in special waters,

Zeus, ruler of the gods

drank from a holy well and inhaled the scent of burning laurel leaves (Apollo's symbol) before giving her pronouncements from behind a curtain in the temple's inner sanctum.

The gods also communicated their will to humans by means of signs in the world around them. As a result, everything from the weather and the night sky, through the movements of birds and animals to the patterns made by the intestines of specially sacrificed gutted animals, was fodder for special priestly interpretations.

Specially gifted seers were also blessed with the power to foretell the will of the gods and the future. The most famous of these was Cassandra, the soothsayer who warned the unsuspecting Trojans that their horse-gift from the Greeks was a trick. But Apollo had already cursed Cassandra so that no one believed her future-telling. The city was breached and destroyed.

Festivals Like the Egyptians, the Greeks staged festival celebrations in which the god's cult statue was brought out and carried among the worshippers. But unlike Egypt, the purpose was not to determine the god's intent – instead, the purpose was to placate or please them so they would look favourably on particular projects – the next harvest, a coming battle, or any special forthcoming event.

The social nature of religious festivals and the gods' expected participation in human affairs were well illustrated by the huge five-day festival at Olympia, the greatest in Greece, held in honour of Zeus. The god was believed to have founded the games to commemorate a wrestling match in which he beat his father Cronus to win domination of the gods, and the gods were believed to have taken part in the games. These were the forerunner of the modern-day Olympic Games, dating officially from 776 BC. Messengers were sent to every corner of the region to announce the festival dates. Even wars traditionally stopped to let delegates attend from all over Greece and its colonies. Sculptures of athletes, politicians and soldiers were sent by different regions, others were commissioned and made at the site; choirs sang in competition; sacrifices were offered to the gods; and the athletes competed. The country's most important social, political and religious event, it was the place where the Greeks gained true and lasting fame among their countrymen.

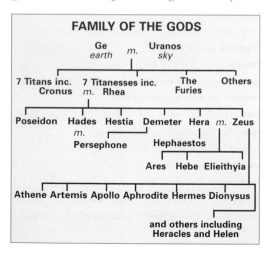

FAMILY OF THE GODS

Ge *earth* m. Uranos *sky*

7 Titans inc. Cronus — 7 Titanesses inc. m. Rhea — The Furies — Others

Poseidon — Hades m. Persephone — Hestia — Demeter — Hera m. Zeus

Hephaestos

Ares — Hebe — Elieithyia

Athene — Artemis — Apollo — Aphrodite — Hermes — Dionysus

and others including Heracles and Helen

The Gods of Olympus

As in Egypt, mythology in Greece evolved over centuries and millenniums, and different gods came to prominence at different times; but for most of the time, twelve gods were thought to reign supreme on Mount Olympus.

THE 12 GODS OF MOUNT OLYMPUS

Zeus chief of the gods

Hera goddess of women and marriage

Poseidon god of the sea

Demeter goddess of the earth and crops

Apollo god of light and fire

Artemis goddess of hunting

Ares god of war

Aphrodite goddess of love and beauty

Hermes messenger of the gods

Athena goddess of wisdom

Hephaestos craftsman of the gods

Dionysus god of wine, fertility and ecstasy

Dionysus supplanted Hestia, goddess of the hearth, by the 5th century BC

ZEUS

Background to Zeus's rise to power

Zeus, ultimate chief of the gods, had an impeccable pedigree. His grandparents were Uranus, the sky and the god of the sky, and Ge, goddess of the Earth, herself born of Chaos. Their children were the Hundred-Handed (the three fifty-headed, hundred-handed giants later appointed guards of Tartarus) and the Cyclopes (one-eyed monsters), and the Titans, destined to be Zeus's opponents in the divine war for supremacy. Uranus kept their children imprisoned in Ge's body, but she encouraged her son Cronus, a Titan, to rise against his father, and he castrated him with a sickle.

Cronus proved just as bad as his father. Being warned in a prophecy that he would be deposed by one of his

---

Zeus's status The sky god; god of rain, storms and thunder; chief of the 12 gods of Olympus

Zeus's family son of Cronus and Rhea; brother of Hades, Poseidon, Hera, Demeter and Hestia; husband of Hera, his sister; father of innumerable gods and humans

Zeus's symbols eagle, oak, thunderbolt, lightning, sceptre

Victor: Zeus crowned by Nike, goddess of Victory

own children, he swallowed each as they were born. But his wife, Rhea, tricked him after the birth of Zeus, their youngest son, by handing him a stone to swallow instead. Zeus grew up in safety on Crete until he grew old enough to confront his father. He persuaded Metis, a sea-goddess, to give Cronus an emetic. This made him vomit up Zeus's siblings who immediately joined their brother in a war against their father and the other Titans. (Cronus also vomited up the stone he had thought was Zeus; it was later set at Delphi – see p. 79 – and known as the omphalos, the navel or centre of the earth.)

Zeus's victory was secured when he descended into Tartarus and freed the Cyclopes to come to his aid. They in turn made a thunderbolt for their liberator, a trident for Poseidon and a cap to make Hermes invisible. The weapons proved decisive and defeat after ten hard-fought years saw Cronus and his family cast into Tartarus, to be guarded by the Hundred-Handed. After their victory Zeus, Poseidon and Hades cast lots to divide up rulership of the world. Poseidon drew the sea, Hades the underworld and Zeus the sky. The three were to share the earth and Olympus.

Zeus produced his own daughter, Athena; she sprang from his head after Hephaestos split it with an axe (see p. 90)

RELATIONS WITH OTHER GODS

As the god of the sky in all its phases, Zeus was just as changeable in his moods and actions. Victory over the Titans established him as head of the gods, and as ruler of Olympus he settled quarrels between fellow deities – for example, in the dispute between Persephone and Aphrodite in their quarrel over the beautiful Adonis, or Apollo's sentence of temporary exile from Olympus for killing the Cyclopes.

RELATIONS WITH HUMANS

As head of the gods, Zeus was regarded as the protector of the state and of Athens. He was vital to crops and the harvest, sending down rain on the earth from heaven. But although he was invoked any time drought delayed the harvest, Zeus was not particularly well-disposed towards humanity: he vented his cruelty by depriving them of the basics of food, heat and light, and punished Prometheus for his compassion in stealing fire from the gods for his human creations. (Zeus bound Prometheus to a rock for 30,000 years; an eagle picked out his liver every day and it regenerated every night. Prometheus was finally rescued by Heracles. He was also, ironically, god of the family and, with his wife Hera (see p. 68), of marriage.

SEXUAL EXPLOITS

Of course, Zeus was also infamous for his obsessive philandering with other deities and mortal women and men. Although Hera was usually called his wife, he was married several times. A huge number of stories catalogue Zeus's trysts and conquests, each more bizarre than the next: how he became a swan to seduce Leda; how he turned into a shower of gold to get to Danaë; and how, as a bull, he carried off Europa.

The story of Europa The beautiful daughter of the Phoenecian King Agenor was abducted from her father's palace gardens by Zeus in the form of a bull. He swam across the sea with her on his back to Crete where she had three sons – Minos, Rhadamanthys and Sarpedon. Minos became king of Crete and later sat with Rhadamanthys in judgement in Hades; Sarpedon was killed in the Trojan War.

Zeus's adoption of any tactic to get a partner is the subject of various poems and stories, such as these lines by the poet Robert Herrick:

> But fables we'll relate, how Jove [Zeus]
> Put on all shapes to get a love,
> As now a satyr, then a swan,
> A bull then, and now a man.

ZEUS'S CULT

The god was worshipped across the ancient world and his main oracle was at Dondona where a sacred oak-tree rustled in the wind to pass Zeus's words and prophecies on to his initiates. His greatest statue by

SOME OF ZEUS'S CHILDREN

- Apollo and Artemis, god of the sun and goddess of the moon
  (Zeus had five other Olympians as his children)

- Athena, goddess of war, wisdom and Athens

- Hermes, messenger of the gods and patron of travellers and thieves

- Dionysus, god of wine and fertility

- Persephone, a goddess of the Underworld

- Aphrodite, goddess of love and beauty (by some accounts)

- The Graces

- The Seasons

- The Fates

- The Muses

- Heracles

- Helen

- Minos, King of Crete

- Perseus, King of Mycenae

Phidias at Olympia was given divine approval when, in answer to the sculptor's prayers, Zeus sent a bolt of lightning to illuminate, but not touch, his statue. Olympia was also the site of the games, held in honour of Zeus's victory over the Titans.

Zeus is at the centre of Greek myth to the extent that his stories would fill a book by themselves. Different aspects of the god can be found in various classical writings: the drama Prometheus Bound by Aeschylus shows the god as tyrant, while Homer's Iliad gives a traditional view of the ruler of the gods.

HERA

HERA'S FAMILY

Like her brothers and sisters, Hera was swallowed by Cronus, their father, until their rescue by Zeus. She was very beautiful, and became Zeus's wife after he took the form of a cuckoo to seduce her. The garden of the gods was the venue for their wedding, and as it took place a wondrous tree bearing fruit of golden apples of the Hesperides sprang up. Their children included Eilethyia, goddess of childbirth, although this role Hera often assumed herself. Two Olympians were her children: Ares, god of war, and Hephaestos, the lame smith-god. Some accounts say jealousy over Zeus's producing Athena himself led her to produce Hephaestos on her own (see p. 94).

Hera's status queen of the gods; goddess of
women, marriage and childbirth.

Hera's family daughter of Cronus and Rhea; sister
of Zeus, Hades, Poseidon, Demeter and Hestia;
wife of Zeus; mother of Ares, Hebe and Eilethyia
by him, as well as Hephaestos and others

Hera's symbols the peacock, cuckoo, crow and the
pomegranate

THE WRATH OF HERA

In fact, jealousy was one of Hera's main motivations
and her cruel and repeated persecutions of anyone
Zeus favoured too much – especially his countless
lovers and their children – feature strongly in her stories. No one, divine or immortal, was immune from
her vengeful wrath. She persecuted the Titan goddess
Leto, mother of Apollo and Artemis, even though
Zeus had fathered them before he had married Hera.

The story of Io One of Hera's own priestesses, Io,
was another of her husband's conquests and Hera's
most famous victims. Zeus changed her into a heifer
to hide her from Hera, but she was suspicious and in
turn sent Argus, her many-eyed servant, to keep watch
on her rival. Argus was killed by Hermes on Zeus's
orders, but Hera, furious at her servant's death, sent a

gadfly to torment Io. (Hera set the eyes of Argus in the tail of her favourite bird, the peacock.) Io, meanwhile, was forced to wander ceaselessly in search of rest from the gadfly's stings, at one point throwing herself into the sea to get away:

> In coming time that hollow of the sea
> Shall bear the name Ionian, and present
> A monument of Io's passage through,
> Unto all mortals.
>
> *Elizabeth Barrett Browning*

Only after she came to Egypt did Hera relent at her husband's request, and let Io return to her own form and have her child.

Two of her most famous mortal victims later became gods themselves: Zeus's son Dionysus was not just persecuted himself; those who helped him were ruined or killed. But Hera's most famous victim was Heracles (*see p. 100*) for whom she devised inventive and ceaseless trials and tortures. In the end Zeus himself was forced to step in to punish her cruelty, hanging her from the heavens with anvils tied to her feet.

It was not just jealousy at her husband's favour that infuriated Hera; she was quick to take offence at any slight, deliberate or unintended.

- Beautiful women incurred her wrath as rivals: the hunter Orion's wife Side was banished to Hades for boasting she was more beautiful than Hera;

- Disrespectful mortals ignored her at their peril: Pelias, king of Iolcus, killed his cruel stepmother as she looked for sanctuary at one of Hera's altars, and always refused to honour the goddess. She in turn helped Jason (see p. 110) come safely to Iolcus with the sorceress Medea, who tricked the king's daughters into murdering their own father;

Hera

- Those judging against her in disputes regretted it: Paris brought about his own death and the destruction of his home city, Troy, after he judged against Hera, and Athene, in a beauty contest against Aphrodite. (See p. 115.)

HERA'S CULT

Hera was worshipped in several forms: along with her daughter Eilethyia she helped women in childbirth; she occasionally took on the form of an old woman or of a girl; but most often it was as a mature woman, as the goddess of marriage and fertility. Her cult was spread across the whole of Greece but she was especially honoured in Argos, Mycenae and Sparta, and her foremost temples were at the Heraeum at Nemea, the temple on Samos and the temple at Olympia. Olympia was also the scene of the Heraean Games, held in honour of the goddess every four years. Predating the Olympic Games, they saw women and girls compete for athletic prizes, with olive garlands presented to the winners.

POSEIDON

POSEIDON'S BACKGROUND

One of the three Olympian brothers who drew lots for dominion over the earth, Poseidon won overlordship of the sea while Hades got the Underworld and Zeus the sky. Poseidon was not the only god of the sea and waters, but as an Olympian he was the most powerful. More minor gods, often the children of the Titans Oceanus and Tethys, oversaw the rivers but Poseidon had jurisdiction over the salt waters, fresh waters and the springs that came out of the earth.

He lived with his wife, Amphitrite, in a golden palace on the sea bottom and moved through his kingdom in a golden chariot pulled by golden-hooved, brass-maned horses. The seas were calmed as he rode, but he could equally throw up storms and wreck ships. He had

Poseidon's status god of the sea – notably the
   Mediterranean and Black Seas – earthquakes
   and of horses

Poseidon's family son of Cronus and Rhea; brother of Zeus, Hades, Hera, Demeter and Hestia;
   husband of Amphitrite; father of Amyous,
   Antaeus, Arion, Pegasus, Polyphemus, Theseus,
   Triton, Rhode and others

Poseidon's symbols the horse, trident, dolphin

many children: with his wife, two daughters, Rhode
and Benthesicyme, and a son, the sea-god Triton, half-
fish, half man, who could calm the seas by blowing
through a conch-shell. Other liaisons produced
numerous offspring, including mortals like Theseus,
king of Athens and slayer of the Cretan Minotaur (*see
p. 107*) and even several of the Argonauts (*see p. 111*).
As the god of horses, he also numbered some among
his children: he had sex with Demeter, his sister, while
he was in the form of a horse and she bore a horse-
child, Arion. And Poseidon's affair with Medusa also
produced one of the most wonderful creatures in
Greek myth. The god seduced the young, beautiful
Medusa in the temple of Athena, moving the war

Temple of Poseidon

goddess to rage and a terrible punishment: she turned Medusa's hair into writhing snakes and her face so horrible that people turned to stone when they saw it. Medusa the Gorgon was later beheaded by Perseus (*see p. 104*) but from two drops of blood that fell from her neck came her two children by Poseidon: the warrior, Chrysaor, and Pegasus, the winged horse.

STORIES OF POSEIDON

Although his youngest brother was the overall ruler, Poseidon did not always welcome Zeus's authority and once joined in rebellion with Hera and Athena. Exiled to earth by his brother as punishment, he was ordered to build the walls of Troy for King Laomedon who promised him a great reward. But promises were easier made than kept, and Laomedon was foolish enough to go back on his word. His avarice was punished with a monster sent by Poseidon which devoured everything on the shore and was only appeased by the sacrifice on the rocks of a beautiful virgin of Troy. (*See Heracles, p. 102.*) The Trojans also earned Poseidon's unremitting enmity in their war with the Greeks.

Poseidon also had a famous dispute with Athena over who should be patron of the beautiful new city of Attica. Zeus passed the judgement (and the buck) to the city authorities who were persuaded by the benefits each god offered: Poseidon produced a horse, Athena an olive tree. The horse was a symbol of war, the olive tree of peace – besides having many other uses – and that was what the judges chose, with the goddess giving her name to the city. The gods' contest is featured on the west pediment of the Parthenon.

POSEIDON'S CULT

Poseidon was worshipped across the Greek lands, with a particular following in the coastal areas and islands such as Delos and Crete, where he was often the patron.

Poseidon's trident symbol

DEMETER

DEMETER'S STORY

The story of Demeter and her daughter Persephone, goddess of vegetation, is one of the best known in ancient Greek mythology, and one where a deity is portrayed, unusually, as faithful and loving.

Hades, god of the Underworld, had tried long and unsuccessfully to find a wife but no one wanted to leave the earth for the sunless Underworld. Struck by Persephone's beauty when he saw her in a garden, and with Zeus's collusion, Hades kidnapped her to his kingdom. In the evening Demeter returned to look for her daughter, but the search stretched on for days with no success. Her work was left undone, and crops were neglected and died as she wandered in search of Persephone.

Disguised as an old woman, she visited many towns as

she searched. One of the most famous was Eleusis where the daughters of King Celeus took pity on her and brought her back to their palace where she was employed as nurse to the king's baby son. Demeter loved the baby, and to make him immortal, anointed him with ambrosia and put him to sleep in the fire at night to burn out all mortality from him. But the queen, checking on her son, discovered his terrifying bed and seized him out. Demeter at once transformed into her divine appearance and reproached the queen that her son must now remain mortal forever. Demeter taught the Eleusinians the proper rites of her worship and stayed in the temple they built for her.

Meanwhile, without Demeter and Persephone to tend the crops and vegetation a famine had struck the earth. Zeus and the Olympians were concerned not for humankind, but for themselves: no crops meant

---

Demeter's status goddess of crops, agriculture and the earth's produce, and of fertility

Demeter's family daughter of Cronus and Rhea; sister of Zeus, Hades, Hera, Hestia and Poseidon; mother of Persephone (by Zeus), Plutus and Philomelus

Demeter's symbols a sheaf of barley or wheat, fruit, honeycomb, cow and sow

humans would die out and there would be no sacrifices to the gods. Despite their pleas Demeter refused to budge without her daughter, and Zeus eventually despatched Hermes to fetch Persephone. But before she left his domain, Hades offered Persephone pomegranate seeds, the fruit of the Underworld, for the journey. By eating them, Persephone condemned herself to spend at least four months of the year with Hades. Demeter eventually accepted the situation, but when her daughter left her each winter, the goddess left plants to wither and die in her sadness and loss.

DEMETER'S CULT

King Celeus's son learned from Demeter how to grow grain and he taught both that message and the rites of her cult. Athens's dominance meant that Demeter's cult at Eleusis, which was near the city, spread far and wide across Greece.

APOLLO

APOLLO'S BIRTH

Apollo and his twin sister Artemis were born on the island of Delos in the Cyclades, in the teeth of opposition from the jealous Hera who did everything in her power to harass their pregnant mother.

THE ORACLE AT DELPHI

When, according to some accounts, Apollo was only days old, he killed the snake Python that lived at the

Delphi

Delphi oracle. In later years he returned to Delphi and made the oracle, previously owned by Gaea, the earth goddess, his own. The whole island was deemed sacred and the oracle became the most popular in Greece.

APOLLO'S ATTRIBUTES

Part of the power of the Delphi oracle came from Apollo's status as the god of prophecy. As the sun god, he drove his solar chariot across the sky each day. He was a skilled archer and was also the god of music. He sang songs and was usually depicted with a lyre, an instrument he played without parallel. He was the leader of the Muses – the nine daughters of Zeus who inspired all artists – and was proud and defensive of

> ***Apollo's status*** god of the sun, prophesy, healing,
>   archery, music and youth
>
> ***Apollo's family*** son of Zeus and the Titan goddess
>   Leto; twin sister of Artemis
>
> ***Apollo's symbols*** lyre, bow; laurel tree and bay
>   leaf, palm tree; wolf, dolphin, hawk, crow and
>   snake

his skill, too: when King Midas of Phrygia declared that the goat- or shepherd-god Pan, who played on his pipes, was a better musician, Apollo changed his ears into the ears of an ass. He was also the god of healing and medicine. Some of his children inherited Apollo's traits, and there were many stories of them.

One of the most notable inheritors of his father's gifts was Asclepius, a compassionate physician of near-miraculous skill. His ultimate act was to bring a dead man to life again, but this was an upstart step too far for his grandfather, Zeus, who struck him dead with a thunderbolt. Apollo took out his revenge on the thunderbolt makers, the Cyclopes, by killing them with his arrows. His mother Leto's intervention was all that saved Apollo from being thrown into Tartarus by his livid father; instead his sentence was commuted to a year's exile from Olympus, to work for a mortal master.

STORIES OF APOLLO

The mortal Apollo worked for on earth was King Admetus of Thessaly, whom he rewarded for his kind treatment by helping him win Alcestis, daughter of King Pelias. But soon afterwards the king became mortally ill and Apollo pleaded with the Fates (*see p. 56*) to spare his life. They agreed on condition that someone else would give their life in return. None of Admetus's fawning courtiers or brave warriors was willing: the only volunteer was his new wife, Alcestis, and before the king could stop her, she was taken by Thanatos (Death). But Heracles arrived at Admetus's palace soon after and challenged Thanatos to a wrest-

Apollo

ling match for the life of the queen. Heracles won and Alcestis was restored to life and her husband.

During his time on earth Apollo also helped Poseidon build up the walls of Troy (see p. 74), sitting himself on rocks near the work and playing music so sweet that the stones moved into place by themselves.

Love affairs Apollo's powers of goodness were manifested in his appearance – from an early age he was the most beautiful of all the gods and he had many lovers. But many of the most famous were either unsuccessful or ended in tragedy. Daphne, a water-nymph, chose to be changed into a laurel tree rather than become his lover. The laurel became Apollo's sacred tree.

But he was not so generous to another woman who refused his advances. Cassandra was the daughter of King Priam of Troy, and was one of Apollo's priestesses. Apollo bribed her to become his lover, giving her the gift of prophecy. When she refused, he cursed her so that her prophecies would never be believed. Cassandra foretold the destruction of Troy, warning of the Greeks hiding inside the wooden horse, but her prophecies of doom for the city always fell on unbelieving ears. Tragedy dogged her for the rest of her life.

Apollo's male lovers did no better: Hyacinthus was killed accidentally, either by Zephyrus, the west wind, who also loved him, or by Apollo himself. The blood that fell from Hyacinthus's wounds was changed into flowers by Apollo. Cyparissus, another man Apollo loved, chose to grieve forever after he accidentally killed a beloved pet stag. After his death Apollo changed him into a cypress tree which he said should always shelter the graves of those beloved in life.

Apollo's positive force as a god of the light was long an inspiration to artists and poets; these lines come from Shelley's *Hymn to Apollo*:

> I am the eye with which the Universe
> Beholds itself and knows itself divine;
> All harmony of instrument or verse,
> All prophecy, all medicine are mine,
> All light of art or nature; to my song
> Victory and praise in its own right belong.

ARTEMIS

ARTEMIS'S STORY

As Apollo's chariot pulled the sun across the sky by day, so Artemis was goddess of the moon. She was also the goddess of the hunt, and most of her stories concern that attribute. Young women who were virgins like herself, were her hunting companions. One of the stories of Artemis tells of how she fell in love with Orion, a giant of a young man who hunted with her on Crete along with his dog, Sirius. Apollo disapproved of his sister's intention to marry, and one day while they hunted together near the shore, he saw Orion swimming far off in the water. He wagered his sister that she could not hit the black object in the sea with an arrow. Artemis took on the challenge and won the bet, but was appalled when her lover's body washed ashore, an arrow through his head. To commemorate and honour him, Orion and his dog were placed among the stars. (Many of the stars were individuals who had featured in the lives of the gods.)

Artemis was effective at warding off unwanted advances,

> **Artemis's status** goddess of the moon, of hunting
> and of wild animals; patron of young women
> and expectant mothers
>
> **Artemis's family** daughter of Zeus and the Titan
> goddess Leto, twin sister of Apollo
>
> **Artemis's symbols** cypress tree, deer, dog

however. Some attackers she herself speared with
arrows, others were tricked or transformed, usually
fatally for them. Any disrespect shown her in other
ways was punished, too: when Agamemnon boasted
that he hunted as well as Artemis, the goddess
brought storms to detain the king's fleet in port and
demanded the sacrifice of his favourite daughter to
make good the insult.

ARTEMIS'S CULT

The huntress was famous as a virgin goddess, but in
her most famous temple at Ephesus her image was
many-breasted – depicting her status as a mother goddess. This association was echoed in her otherwise
apparently incongruous patronage of pregnant
women.

APHRODITE

APHRODITE'S PARTNERS

The capricious, proud and beautiful love goddess was married to the smith-god Hephaestos but she was not faithful to him, or any other partner. Aphrodite's divine partner of choice was Ares, the war god: he came to her when her husband went down from Olympus. A tip-off to the cuckolded Hephaestos eventually ended their affair; he trapped the pair in bed and held them captive for the other gods to ridicule. Aphrodite and Ares had several children, including a daughter, Hermione, and Cupid, the god of love. Her other divine children included Priapus with Dionysus, and Hermaphroditus by Hermes.

Aphrodite

APHRODITE'S STORIES

Mockery and capriciousness were central to Aphrodite's character. She was said to delight in making the other gods fall in love with

> *Aphrodite's status* goddess of sensual love and
> beauty
>
> *Aphrodite's family* daughter of Zeus and Dione,
> by most accounts, although others said she was
> born out of the sea; wife of Hephaestos and
> mother of many children by many fathers
>
> *Aphrodite's symbols* dolphin, dove, rose, ram,
> sparrow

humans, then laughing at them, and any mortal or god
who crossed her might expect to find themselves suddenly infatuated with the most unsuitable partner. The
Graces – usually three in number – helped her, making women beautiful and doling out grace and gentle-
ness wherever they were needed. To further help her,
she had a golden belt which made her irresistible and
anyone she cast a spell on, utterly infatuated with their
beloved. Aphrodite herself was not immune to unsuitable love affairs: one of her most famous loves was
Adonis, a beautiful man who cared as much for hunting as he did for her. But on one particular hunt
Adonis was fatally wounded by a boar and Aphrodite
had to console herself by making blood-red anemones
grow where his blood spilled.

Aphrodite was jealous of her honour and her looks:
any beautiful mortal woman might expect spiteful
treatment. Even when her own son, Cupid, fell in love
with the beautiful Psyche, Aphrodite did everything
she could to prevent the match and only Zeus's inter-
cession allowed the lovers to be together. And jealousy
to guard her status as the most beautiful goddess led
her to bribe Paris in her contest with Athena and
Hera, and to bring about the Trojan War (see p. 115).
Yet she did try to help lovers, and Pygmalion, one of
the kings of Cyprus, was proof that Aphrodite could
help mortals as well as plague them. He sculpted a
statue of his ideal mate, and fell in love with it. His
prayers to Aphrodite to give her life were answered,
and Pygmalion and Galatea were married.

ARES

ARES'S CHILDREN

Although he had no wife, Ares had many children and
some of them – notably Phobus (Alarm) and Deimus
(Fear) – shared his taste for strife. These two warlike
sons were their father's constant companions, often
driving his chariot in battle.

Ares's status god of war

Ares's family son of Zeus and Hera, unmarried

Ares's symbols spear, burning torch, dogs, vulture

ARES'S CHARACTERISTICS

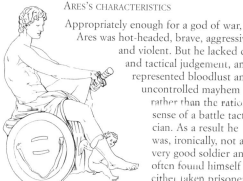

Appropriately enough for a god of war, Ares was hot-headed, brave, aggressive and violent. But he lacked cool and tactical judgement, and represented bloodlust and uncontrolled mayhem rather than the rational sense of a battle tactician. As a result he was, ironically, not a very good soldier and often found himself either taken prisoner or on the losing side. Heracles beat him four times in straight fight

Ares in untypically peaceful pose with Eros, his son

or open battle; Athena defeated him when he took her on over a grudge; and even the young giants Otus and Ephialtes captured and kept him prisoner in a jar for fifteen months until Hermes managed to free him.

The dubious distinction of being the defendant in the first ever murder trial also belonged to Ares. The god killed Halirrhothius, Poseidon's son, for abducting his daughter Alcippe near the Acropolis in Athens. Poseidon had him charged with murder and he stood trial at a hill in Athens later called the Areopagus (Hill of Ares), after the god. He was cleared of the charge.

ATHENA

ATHENA'S BIRTH

Zeus's strong and martial daughter had a most unusual birth, produced from her father's own body. Zeus swallowed her mother, Metis, whole, after a prediction that if Metis had a boy he would rule heaven. When the time came for the child to be born, Zeus suffered an unbearable headache. Either Prometheus or Hephaestos helped him out of his predicament by splitting open his head with an axe, letting a fully armoured and armed Athena leap out. (*See p. 64.*)

ATHENA'S CHARACTERISTICS

Although a war goddess, Athena represented the reverse side of the aggressive, hot-headedness of Ares and significantly, she was able to beat him in almost all of their battles. Instead, she offered wise counsel

---

Athena's status goddess of wisdom, war, arts and
crafts

Athena's family daughter of Zeus; she sprang,
fully armed, from his head after he had swallowed her mother, Metis. Athena herself was a
virgin and had no children

Athena's symbols olive tree, owl

and just cause in war. Heracles she helped several times, as she did others facing difficult tasks in war or adversity, such as Perseus when he faced the Gorgon Medusa, and Odysseus throughout his wanderings.

As well as being a war goddess, Athena was a patron of arts and crafts. One of her most famous stories concerned Arachne, a weaver who boasted of her skills and whom Athena ultimately took on in a contest. Her defeated and devastated opponent hanged herself, only to have the goddess change her into a spider, destined to weave her web endlessly. Athena was also the patron of Athens, site of her most famous temple: the Parthenon, set on the Acropolis. On the same hilltop were the Erechtheum, built on the site of her contest with Poseidon (*see p. 75*) – it sheltered her famous olive tree and housed a wooden statue of her said to have fallen from the heavens in ancient times. Also on the Acropolis was a temple of Athene Nike (the Victorious); and the bronze statue of Athena Promachus, so huge that on a clear day it could be seen by sailors out at sea.

Athena

Hermes's status messenger of the gods; patron of travellers and thieves; guide of dead souls to Hades; god of athletic competitions

Hermes's family son of Zeus and Maia; father of many children by several mothers, including the god Pan; and Hermaphroditus by Aphrodite

Hermes's symbols winged sandals and hat

HERMES

HERMES'S CHARACTERISTICS

The precociousness and cunning at the heart of Hermes's personality were evident from the moment of his birth. While just hours old he stole cattle belonging to Apollo, craftily hiding the evidence, and when he was found out, distracted Apollo from anger by playing beautifully on a lyre he had made out of a tortoiseshell and some sheep-gut. (By some accounts, this was Apollo's first encounter with the instrument he went on to make his own.)

As the herald of Zeus, one of Hermes's duties was to go with his father when he came down from Olympus to earth. A famous story of the two gods told of their visit to Phrygia, an inhospitable land where no one

Hermes

would give the disguised travellers shelter. The only door opened to them was at a poor hut on the hilly outskirts of a town where an old couple, Philemon and Baucis, gave them their own food to eat. But during the meal, as the wine jug kept refilling itself, the hosts suspected their visitors were not mere mortals. When the gods revealed themselves, they flooded the unwelcoming town in the valley with a lake and turned their hosts' hut into a temple, where Philemon and Baucis could live on as keepers. Zeus offered the pair any wish, but what they chose was simply to die together in the same instant. Their wish was granted years later and at the moment of their deaths one became an oak and the other a lime tree, growing together.

HEPHAESTOS

HEPHAESTOS'S FAMILY

Cursed with one of the most dysfunctional families imaginable, Hephaestos justifiably chose to spend much of his time far from Olympus. He was the child either of Hera alone, or of Zeus and Hera together. His first violent exit from Olympus came either when his mother threw him to earth because he was not beautiful, or because he tried to help Hera when she was fighting with her husband. He took a day to fall from the skies onto the island of Lemnos but the fall made him lame. Bad luck dogged him in his choice of wife, too, as he was married to the chronically unfaithful Aphrodite.

HEPHAESTOS'S CRAFTS

His smithy was by some accounts in the heavens, by others under Mount Etna in Sicily, with his forge accounting for the volcano's constant smoking. With the Cyclopes, Hephaestos made armour and weapons for the gods as well as other, more

> ***Hephaestos's status*** god of fire and metalwork-
> ing; craftsman of the gods
>
> ***Hephaestos's family*** son of Hera alone, or else of
> Zeus and Hera; husband of Aphrodite and father
> of various children by various mothers
>
> ***Hephaestos's symbols*** fire

ingenious creations. One of the most famous, built to punish his mother, was a golden throne which held its sitter tight and would not let her get up again. Various gods, including Zeus, asked him to release Hera and come back to Olympus, but it was only when Dionysus got him drunk that he finally agreed.

Hephaestos didn't work just in base metals: he was also skilled in fashioning the finest objects and works of art with the most delicate of tools. He built gold palaces for each of the gods on Olympus, and on earth one of his most notable creations was Pandora, the first woman. She was built at Zeus's request, a troublemaker to counterbalance the compassionate Prometheus. And just as blame was apportioned in the Garden of Eden, so Pandora was responsible for loosing all sorts of evils on the earth by dint of her own failings; only hope was kept back to inspire humans.

DIONYSUS

DIONYSUS'S BIRTH

The last god to join the Olympian set, Dionysus was a deity whose birth was just a bit out of the ordinary. His mother, Semele, was another of Zeus's extra-marital partners who was victimised by Hera. At Hera's suggestion, Semele asked Zeus show her his full divine appearance. Zeus had promised any favour and had to agree, burning the poor woman with the force of a furnace in the process. But he saved their unborn child, snatching him from her dead body and implanting him safely in his own leg until his time came to be born. Hera's persecution, however, continued: she tormented his nurses, had him kidnapped by pirates and sent him mad.

DIONYSUS'S TRAVELS

Dionysus journeyed far and wide, teaching vine culti-vation and wine-making, as well as his own cult, as he

---

Dionysus's status god of vegetation, fertility and wine

Dionysus's family son of Zeus and Semele; hus-band of Ariadne and father of various children

Dionysus's symbols thyrsus (ivy-and-grape-entwined staff, topped by a fir-cone)

went. Hundreds of people were either helped and rewarded as he went, or punished for not recognising his divinity. Among those he encountered in Phrygia was King Midas, who was granted any wish he wanted in return for his kind treatment. To have everything he touched turn to gold was a request that Dionysus granted only reluctantly, and when the starving king soon could not eat, the god advised him to wash away his golden touch in the River Pactolus. Always after that, the river flowed over golden sands. Ariadne, who later became his wife, was another the god met on his travels, and they had several children together.

DIONYSUS'S CULT

A licentious group of assorted satyrs and maenads accompanied Dionysus as he went, unsettling locals with their excessive, orgiastic rites that involved much wine-drinking, music and dancing. The god punished those who did not honour his divinity – often by driving them mad temporarily – possibly a metaphor for drunkenness. His main cult centre was at Thebes.

HESTIA

> *Hestia's status* goddess of the hearth
>
> *Hestia's family* daughter of Cronus and Rhea; sister of Zeus, Hera, Demeter, Poseidon and Hades; she never married and remained a virgin
>
> *Hestia's symbol* hearth

The only Olympian voluntarily to relinquish her position, and the only one guaranteed to receive a welcome wherever she went, Hestia was guardian of the hearth or fireplace and, by extension, the home itself. She turned down marriage proposals from Apollo and Poseidon and stayed aloof from the other gods' quarrels; consequently, there were few stories of her life.

HADES

A child of Cronus and Rhea, and nominally co-equal with Zeus and Poseidon, Hades actually spent very little time on Olympus, preferring to stay in his dark Underworld. In fact, he left his land so infrequently that there are few stories of him; the best known relates his abduction of Persephone, Demeter's daughter (*see p. 76*).

To avoid confusion with the god's realm of Hades, and to avoid naming him for fear of attracting his attention, the Greeks usually called this deity Pluto. No temples were dedicated to him, he had few statues, and at any of his sacrifices, only black animals were offered up.

Hades's status god of the underworld

Hades's family son of Cronus and Rhea; brother

of Zeus, Hera, Demeter, Poseidon and Hestia;

husband of Persephone

Hades's symbols cypress, narcissus

Heroes & Others from Greek Myth

Deities, semi-deities and mortals of divine descent were ten a penny in ancient Greece thanks to the gods' interrelation with each other and with humans. This rich background helped the Greeks weave one of the most colourful tapestries of mythology, and stories of some better known non-divine figures are detailed here.

HERACLES

As much the personification of Greek mythology as
Zeus himself, the hero Heracles (the more familiar
name Hercules is the Romanised version) was one of its
single most important characters. There was hardly
another figure from the mythology who didn't come
into contact with him through his extraordinary saga.

YOUNG HERACLES

As a son of Zeus, Heracles earned the bitter and committed hatred of Hera. After a failed attempt to stop
his mother giving birth to him and his mortal twin,
Iphicles, Hera sent two snakes to kill both babies; the
infant Heracles strangled them with his tiny hands. She
ensured he was subject to another of Zeus's descendants, Eurystheus, King of Mycenae. And after Heracles
married Megara, daughter of King Creon, Hera drove
him mad, causing him to murder his wife and children.
In atonement, after he regained his sanity he was sentenced by the Delphi Pythia to carry out 12 apparently
impossible tasks set by his cousin, Eurystheus.

THE 12 LABOURS OF HERACLES

1 **To kill the lion of Nemea** This fearsome lion could
   not be wounded but Heracles strangled it and took
   its skin to wear as a trophy. This frightened King
   Eurystheus so much that he always hid in a jar any
   time he saw Heracles after that.

2 To kill the Hydra This many headed serpent had the unfortunate characteristic of growing two heads to replace any one cut off. Heracles killed it with help from his nephew and charioteer, Iolaüs, and took its gall to use as poison for his arrows.

3 To capture alive the Cerynitian Hind Famed for its speed and golden horns, it was sacred to Artemis. Heracles took a year to capture it

4 To capture alive the boar of Mount Erymanthus He trapped the huge, ferocious boar in deep snow. He then travelled with the Argonauts for several years before returning to his tasks.

5 To clean out the stables of Augeias Heracles washed out the muck-encrusted land by diverting a river through it.

6 To kill the flesh-eating birds of Lake Stymphalos Heracles made a din with a rattle to scare the birds then shot huge numbers as they flew away.

7 To bring back the Cretan bull This bull was the father of the Minotaur on Crete.

8 To bring back the horses of Diomedes On his way to perform this task, Heracles stopped at the court of Admetus and successfully fought Death for his wife, Alcestis (*see p. 81*). He captured the flesh-eating mares, feeding their master the brutal Diomedes to them in passing.

THE LABOURS OF HERACLES (CONT.)

9 To bring back the belt of Hippolyte, Queen of the Amazons Hippolyte promised Heracles her belt, but Hera tricked the queen's followers into attacking Heracles's ship, with resulting loss of life, including that of the queen. On the way back he stopped at Troy to rescue Princess Hesione, intended as sacrifice to a sea-monster (*see p. 75*).

10 To bring back the cattle of Geryon Geryon was king of Erythrea (now in Andalucia). Heracles travelled through North Africa and set up two pillars, one at Gibraltar and one at Ceuta in Morocco to show how far he had come. The Pillars of Hercules are still so called. After a long, hard journey, Heracles returned with the cows.

11 To bring back the apples of the Hesperides and kill their dragon guardian En route, Heracles freed Prometheus (*see p. 65*) and killed his eagle tormentor. He was tricked by Atlas, the giant who supported the sky, into taking on his burden but tricked him in return, to escape with the apples. He killed the dragon and stopped on his way back to save the Argonauts in the Libyan Desert.

12 To bring back Cerberus, Hades's three-headed dog guardian Cerberus was brother of the Hydra and the Nemean Lion. Heracles fought his way through the Underworld and brought the dog back with or without Hades's permission.

Heracles was promised immortality if he was successful but while still on earth he had to endure many tribulations, usually caused by Hera. When she drove him mad again his victim this time was the honourable son of Eurytus, the King of Oechalia, a crime that saw the Pythia condemn him to three years' slavery. As he travelled home at the end of his punishment he found the body of Icarus, buried it and gave the boy's name to the island, Icaria, where he lay.

AGEING HERACLES

Old scores had to be settled after Heracles' tasks were over and his subsequent visiting of devastation and destruction on good and evil alike that he had met on his travels would fill a book in themselves. But one particular city's history was changed forever by his vengeance: he revisited Troy, where Hesione's father Laomedon had refused his promised reward. Heracles and his men were utterly victorious. Out of the Trojan royal family, only Hesione was allowed to live, though at her request Heracles let her brother Podarces, later called Priam, succeed his father. And Heracles's lieutenant, Telamon, was gifted by Zeus with a brave son, Ajax, for his help to Heracles. Zeus, meanwhile, punished Hera for her persistent persecution of his son by hanging her out of Heaven with anvils tied to her feet.

Heracles himself finally came to grief when the Hydra's poison with which he had tipped his arrows was inadvertently put on his own cloak. He built his own funeral pyre and was received into Olympus by his father, Zeus. He was also, astonishingly, reconciled to his enemy Hera, and married her daughter, Hebe.

Heracles's 12 tasks were depicted at Zeus's temple at Olympia. In completing them, Heracles had roamed as far as the ends of the known world, taken on the most feared creatures of the day, defied the queen of heaven and come back alive from Hades itself. His fame among the Greeks rested not just on these fantastic feats, but because he had spanned the hitherto unbridgeable gulf between mortal and god.

PERSEUS

Another favourite Greek mortal and star of one of the best-known myths was Perseus, slayer of the Gorgon. Like Heracles, Perseus was a son of Zeus.

PERSEUS'S QUEST

King Acrisius of Argos set his daughter Danaë and her baby, Perseus, adrift on the sea after a prophesy foretold her child would kill him; but the pair were washed ashore at Seriphos. For years the island was their home until the king, Polydectes, decided he wanted to marry Danaë, and sent Perseus – who stood in the way of the marriage – to bring him the head of the Gorgon Medusa (see p. 73), part of a fearsome three-headed flying monster whose gaze turned an onlooker to stone.

Perseus had the patronage of Athena, on whose advice

Medusa, as depicted on an ancient piece of pottery

he visited the Graeae, two sisters of the Gorgons, grey since birth, who had one tooth and one eye between them. Perseus stole the eye as it passed between them, forcing them to tell where he could find winged sandals to fly and a cap of darkness to turn him invisible. Kitted out with these, a leather shoulder bag, his shield and a sword from Hermes, he was equipped to face the Gorgon and live.

Wearing his cap and using his shield as a reflective

mirror, Perseus cut off Medusa's head while her two sisters slept and stuffed it into his bag before flying off.

En route home he flew over the land of King Cephus. Cephus's boastful wife Cassiopeia had declared herself more beautiful than any sea-nymph, and by way of punishment Poseidon sent a sea-monster to ravage the land. Only the sacrifice of the king's daughter, Andromeda, left out to be killed on the cliffs, would appease the beast. This was the sight that Perseus saw as he passed. In return for a promise of her hand in marriage, he flew down and killed the monster. The hero also had to see off another of Andromeda's suitors, using Medusa's head to turn him to stone, before he and Andromeda could carry on their journey.

THE HERO RETURNS

At Seriphos he found that in his absence Polydectes had forcibly married Danaë. In fury he marched into the king's hall to announce he had kept his promise – and pulled out the Gorgon's head, turning the king and his followers to stone. With his wife and mother, Perseus then set out for Argos where his grandfather still lived. He had returned his sword to Hermes and gifted Medusa's head to Athena, who ever afterwards had it mounted in the centre of her shield. Perseus bore his callous grandfather no grudge, but the old man fled from such a conquering hero in any case. Perseus caught up with him at the site of some games but tragedy took a hand when Perseus took part in the discus competition: his grandfather was mortally wounded when he stepped in the way of Perseus's discus. So the prophesy was fulfilled.

Unusually for a Greek myth, Perseus and Andromeda lived long and peacefully and were honoured after death by Athena, who placed them among the stars.

THESEUS

THESEUS'S BIRTHRIGHT

Perseus was the great hero of Argos; Theseus played that role in Athens. Theseus's father was either King Aegeus of Athens, or Poseidon. To claim his birthright in his mortal father's city he travelled overland from Troezen, overcoming on the way an imaginative variety of fearsome villains, including Corynetes the Clubman who clubbed unwary travellers to death; Pityocamptes the Pine-bender who catapulted people into the air atop bent-down pine trees which were suddenly released; the savage sow of Crommyon; Sceiron, a giant who fed unsuspecting travellers to a giant turtle; and Procrustes, an apparently hospitable innkeeper who cut or stretched his overnight guests to fit his bed.

Once in Athens, and after more scrapes, Theseus was happily acknowledged by Aegeus as his son. But their meeting was destined to be short-lived. Many years before Athens had lost a war to Crete, whose king, Minos, was now entitled to demand nine-yearly tribute from the city of seven boys and seven girls, to be sacrificed to the savage Minotaur, the half-man, half-bull that lived in Minos's Labyrinth on Crete. Theseus volunteered to be one of the 14 young people who set off for Crete. His father made the party promise that if Theseus returned alive, their ship should fly a white flag, but if, as expected, he were dead, a black flag should fly from the mast.

THESEUS V THE MINOTAUR

Celebratory games were held before the ritual sacrifice in Crete, and when the king's daughter Ariadne saw Theseus there she fell in love with him. Knowing he was destined to die, she went for help to Daedalus, designer of the Labyrinth. On his advice Ariadne gave Theseus a ball of string to tie to the maze entrance and unroll as he passed through. He killed the Minotaur with his bare hands before retracing his steps. With Ariadne, the Athenians fought their way back to their ships, although Theseus abandoned the princess on his way home (Ariadne was said then to have killed herself in despair, or to have married Dionysus). Sadly for Aegeus, Theseus forgot his promise to fly a white flag, and returned home to find that his father had killed himself in grief, leaving him king of Athens.

KING OF ATHENS

Theseus proved a model ruler, finally uniting Athens and its neighbouring towns under one rule and defeating the various factions and rivals to his father's

DAEDALUS & ICARUS

Daedalus was an Athenian master craftsman in exile on Crete for the murder of his talented nephew apprentice. He was employed there by King Minos, but his strangest royal job was the building of a Labyrinth, an impenetrable maze of a building to hide the Minotaur, hideous bestial offspring of Queen Pasiphaë's infatuation with a bull.

At Ariadne's request Daedalus helped Theseus find his way out of the Labyrinth, to the fury of Minos who imprisoned him and Icarus, his son. But Daedalus had already prepared his escape: he made two sets of wax and feather wings, for himself and Icarus, which they used to fly away from Crete.

Daedalus warned Icarus not to fly too low, where the sea-spray would wet and clog his feathers, or too high, where the sun would melt the wax. But as they flew over the sea Icarus forgot the warning and, flying too near the sun, saw the wax binding his wings melt before he plummeted out of the sky into the Aegean.

Daedalus flew on to land, finding a lasting refuge in Sicily.

throne. But in later life his pursuit of power and exploits with young women and children led him to abandon his kingdom; he even found himself imprisoned in Hades for several years, and was only rescued by Heracles as he passed through. He ended his life in exile, and it was long after his death that he was rehabilitated as the hero-king and unifier of his city.

JASON AND THE ARGONAUTS

Like Pericles, Jason was another hero who made good after someone plotted to get him out of the way. The throne of Iolcus was usurped by Jason's half-uncle Pelias and when Jason was born, his father – the rightful successor – and his mother sent the child away for safety, to be brought up be Cheiron the Centaur.

JASON'S QUEST

Jason eventually returned to claim his father's throne, but was challenged by Pelias to a quest to prove himself – to bring back the golden fleece of a magical ram from faraway Colchis, where it had been taken by Phrixus, a prince of Iolcus; it was now guarded by a dragon that never slept. Jason agreed to the challenge and, taking young nobles from all over Greece, set out in a ship called the Argo, after Argus, its builder. Argus had been helped in his work by Athena, while Hera also watched over much of the voyage, having her own reasons for seeking the downfall of the disrespectful Pelias.

The Argonauts' adventures These were too many to list here but the following were some of the highlights.

- They visited Lemnos, an island wholly populated by women, and fathered several children, ensuring the island's future
- they killed the six-armed giants of Bear Mountain;
- they saved the seer-king Phileus from the torments of the Harpies (winged female monsters set on him by Zeus for revealing the god's plans for humanity);
- they sailed safely through the ship-crushing Clashing

Jason fighting the warriors that sprang from dragon's teeth, as seen by Hollywood

THE ARGONAUTS: HERACLES

Many of the Argonauts were famous in their own
right; Heracles was one such. He interrupted his
labours part-way through to sail with Jason,
although there was some confusion about his part
in the voyage – all accounts say he was voted cap-
tain, although many say he made way for Jason,
and others still that the magical talking beam on the
Argo complained that it could not carry his weight.
Most accounts state Heracles was left behind early
on. His young squire, Hylas, was stolen away by
some water nymphs, and when Heracles insisted on
searching for him, the ship sailed on without him.

Rocks in the Bosphorus Straits that separated the
Aegean from the Black Sea;

- they overcame all the tests set for them by Aeëtes,
  king of Colchis, in whose land the Golden Fleece
  was, with the help of Medea, the king's sorceress
  daughter – to yoke fire-breathing bulls, plough a
  field with them, sow it with dragon's teeth and kill
  the warriors who sprang up from the teeth;

- with Medea's help they overcame the Fleece's drag-
  on-guardian and took it, as well as Medea herself;

- they treacherously killed Medea's pursuing brother,
  Apsyrtus;

- they successfully sailed past the Sirens whose beautiful songs lured sailors to forgetfulness of all else, and ultimately starvation and death;

- carried the *Argo* on their backs across the Libyan desert sands for nine days to reach the sea;

- and they overcame countless other perils on land and sea to finally come home and see Pelias crushed and killed.

THE ARGONAUTS: CASTOR AND POLYDEUCES

These two sons of Spartan King Tyndareus were called Dioscuri, sons of Zeus; in fact, Polydeuces was alone thought Zeus's son, while Castor was the child of the king. The pair rescued their sister Helen from Theseus after he abducted the child. They themselves were still young when they sailed with the *Argo* and made their names as heroes.

In later years the brothers were involved in cattle-raiding and Castor was killed. Polydeuces pleaded with Zeus to be allowed to share his own immortality with his brother, so that the pair spent every other day on Olympus or in Hades. They were later set in the sky as stars, and were identified with St Elmo's Fire and the constellation Gemini.

THE ARGONAUTS: ORPHEUS

Like Heracles, Orpheus was another famous Argonaut. A superbly skilled musician, his lyre-playing and singing could make stones and trees rise up and follow him. His music calmed the other sailors enough to stop their quarrelling, and he saved the whole crew from the Sirens by drowning out their song.

Orpheus married Eurydice but soon after their marriage she died from a venomous snake-bite. Determined to snatch her back from death, Orpheus went down into the Underworld, playing his lyre as he went. His music was beautiful and moving enough to charm not just the shades and the damned, but Hades and Persephone themselves. They agreed to his request to take his wife back to the land of the living, on condition that he lead her and never turn around until they reached the surface. Orpheus walked on, up to the opening to earth, where his courage failed him. As he turned around to make sure his wife was behind him, Eurydice was snatched back to Hades once again.

Orpheus himself died soon after, killed by women of the Cicones because he stayed faithful to his wife's memory.

Jason was not the greatest leader in Greek mythology; his leadership and his spirits had waxed and waned through the trip, and his fellow Argonauts had to buck him up several times to keep him going. Without Medea's help in Aea and on the return journey, he would never have been successful. And in the end, the kingship for which he had taken on the whole voyage was never to be his – he and Medea were exiled for murdering Pelias.

THE END

There was rarely a happy-ever-after ending to Greek stories, and Jason's was no different. Ambition for power and position caused him to court the daughter of the Corinthian king and, with incredible folly, to divorce Medea so he could take a new wife. Not surprisingly given her past record, Medea took a ferocious revenge: she killed not only Jason's new wife and new father-in-law, but her and Jason's own two children as well. Jason's own end was farcically appropriate rather than tragic: as he sat in a great depression under the wreck of the *Argo*, the vehicle and reminder of his glory days, he was crushed by a rotted falling beam.

THE TROJAN WAR

The small spark that ignited this great battle between the Greeks and the Trojans was a divine beauty contest judged by Paris, prince of Troy and universally agreed to be the world's handsomest mortal. Hera,

Athena and Aphrodite were in dispute over who was the fairest, and of the bribes offered by each, Paris chose Aphrodite's: the love of Helen, the world's most beautiful woman and wife of the king of Sparta. Paris set off for Sparta and took not just the king's wife but also a large part of his treasure.

Menelaüs, Helen's husband, also happened to be the brother of Agamemnon, the Mycenaean warrior-king, and he raised a large Greek force to sail for Troy. Prophecies foretold the Greeks should besiege the walled city for nine years and take it in the tenth, and so it proved. Nine years were spent subduing the Trojans' allies in the surrounding country but despite losing them and most of its leaders, Troy still stood, apparently invincible. Only trickery finally won the war for the Greeks: a large wooden horse was built to conceal troops inside, while the rest of the force left, apparently for home. The surprisingly gullible Trojans took the horse inside the walls and at night, as the city slept, the Greeks came out to open the gates to their now-returned army. They took a terrible toll in their victory, murdering almost the entire Trojan royal family, throwing children from the city walls and slaughtering the inhabitants without mercy. The city was destroyed.

The actions of the gods started the war but although they took sides in the conflict, the most memorable stories were of the actions of mortals. Some of the most famous participants are listed on p. 117–118.

SOME KEY GREEK PLAYERS IN THE TROJAN WAR

Achilles Son of King Peleus and Thetis, a sea-goddess who tried to confer immortality on him. The legend may have arisen because he was one of the Greeks' greatest warriors. When his lover Patroclus, dressed in his armour, was killed by Hector, the enraged Achilles went into a frenzy of killing. He dragged the body of Hector, his greatest victim, three times around the city walls. Paris killed Achilles with a single arrow.

Ajax Another great warrior but one who died in ignominy. Ajax and Odysseus vied for Achilles' armour after his death and Ajax was so distressed at losing that, crazed, he slaughtered the Greeks' animals. When he came to his senses he killed himself in shame at his own actions.

Agamemnon Warrior-king of Mycenae and Helen's brother-in-law. He sacrificed his own daughter to Artemis to allow the Greek ships to set sail at the start of the war. He was murdered by his wife on his return in revenge for their daughter's death.

Odysseus One of the brains behind the Greek victory, Odysseus was the originator of the wooden horse plan. Tales of his craftiness abound but he was also brutal: he insisted on the death of Hector's small son in the killing frenzy after Troy fell. His other adventures are detailed on p. 118.

SOME KEY TROJAN PLAYERS IN THE TROJAN WAR

Hector Trojan military leader, the son of King Priam and brother of Paris. Although he deplored Paris's rash stupidity in kidnapping Helen, he took part wholeheartedly in the war. A forthright and brave soldier, he was killed by Achilles who dishonoured his body, only handing it over for burial when his father the king came to the camp at night to beg for its return.

Priam The last king of Troy. He had wanted to send Paris back with Helen and his booty but his sons refused. Almost all of his children died in the war or its aftermath; Priam himself was killed while seeking sanctuary at the altar of Zeus.

ODYSSEUS

Few of the victorious Greeks had an easy trip home – or indeed managed to get back at all. Probably the most famous of all the return journeys was that of Odysseus, who took ten more years to get back. Storms drove his ten ships off course and set them wandering through one strange land after another.

Odysseus's adventures Like the Argonauts, Odysseus had many adventures, scrapes and near misses.

- Scouts sent ashore into north Africa found the land of the lotus-eaters. The people there were happy just to eat this fruit, take life easy and forget any ambitions. Odysseus had to drag his men away.

- They escaped from the cave of the man-eating Cyclopes on Sicily by getting him drunk then blinding his only eye. The vain Odysseus stupidly taunted the Cyclopes as they sailed away; he in turn pleaded with his father, Poseidon, to make Odysseus's trip and homecoming long and difficult.

- Odysseus's ship alone escaped when his little fleet was set upon by the man-eating Laestrygonian giants; the crews of the other nine ships provided a fine feast for their hosts.

- With the help of Hermes, they overcame the sorceress Circe who transformed people into animals.

- The sailors visited the dead seer Teiresias in Hades, the only one who could advise them how to get home safely.

- They sailed past the Sirens by stopping their ears with melted wax (*see p. 120*) then sailed past the six-headed monster of Scylla which ate six of the crew.

- They ate the sacred sheep of Helios the sun-god on Thrinacia and were punished by a violent storm that wrecked the boat and drowned all but Odysseus.

- He survived several shipwrecks, with the help of the goddess Athena and finally got a lucky break when kindly Phaeacian sailors brought him home.

Odysseus sails past the sirens; as depicted on ancient pottery

He returned home in a beggar's disguise to find his house besieged by suitors for the hand of his wife, Penelope; only his swineherd, Eumaeüs and his old dog, Argus, recognised him. Penelope announced a contest for her hand: the suitors had to shoot an arrow through twelve axes, as her husband could do. The disguised beggar also took part – the only one able to complete the task. A furious battle ensued as Odysseus revealed himself, which ended only when all the suitors were dead. Odysseus established himself as master in his own land again. Although he wandered further again in later years, he died at home at the hands of his son by Circe, defending his lands.

ROMAN MYTHOLOGY

Rome's Religious Myths

FROM GREEK TO ROMAN

The gods and the mythology that we now think of as Roman were lifted in large part straight from ancient Greece – and, to a lesser extent, other cultures. As Rome's influence expanded so the Romans came into contact with, and absorbed, other religions. From the Etruscans they took deities like Ceres, goddess of

Rome and its areas of influence

crops; from Latium, Minerva, Venus and others; and then from southern Italy and Sicily, the gods and the mythology of the Greeks who had first settled in Italy around 750 BC. (*See p. 128.*)

As the table on page 123 shows, there were direct Roman equivalents of the major (and many minor) gods of Greece. Their qualities were duplicated, too, with some modifications along the way. Where there were differences in the two mythologies, this was due in part to the different Roman outlook on life: for example, the Roman versions of the gods did not duplicate the self-serving sensuality of their Greek counterparts. There was also less casual cruelty and tyranny. The stories and mythology were also modified to accommodate the Romans' own rituals.

Worship of the Graeco-Roman gods constituted the state religion, involving strict rituals and elaborate ceremonies which grew in complexity as Rome expanded its territories. People prayed and sacrificed to the gods for whatever favour they wanted. Many had a patron or favourite god; others simply prayed to the god who governed the area of life they wanted to succeed in. As in Greece, temples were built to house the statues of the individual gods and they were looked after by the priests and priestesses. Sacrifices were offered at altars in front of the temple in ceremonies carefully conducted by the priests. Ordinary people could also go into the temple to pray.

ROMAN GODS & GREEK EQUIVALENTS

Roman	Designation	Greek
Jupiter	Ruler of the gods; god of the sky	Zeus
Juno	Goddess of women & mothers; wife of Jupiter	Hera
Neptune	God of the sea	Poseidon
Ceres	Goddess of crops & fertility	Demeter
Apollo	God of healing, music, the arts, prophecy, the sun	Apollo
Diana	Goddess of hunting, animals & the moon	Artemis
Mars	God of war	Ares
Venus	Goddess of love & beauty	Aphrodite
Mercury	Messenger of the gods	Hermes
Minerva	Goddess of wisdom & crafts	Athena
Vulcan	The smith god & armourer; god of craftsmen	Hephaestos
Liber	God of wine, ecstasy & fertility	Dionysus
Vesta	Goddess of the hearth	Hestia
Dis	God of the Underworld	Hades
Cupid	God of love; Venus's son	Eros
Faunus	Woodland god	Pan

PURELY ROMAN GODS

But these major gods of the state religion did not make up the whole pantheon. On an altogether more human scale than Jupiter, Juno and their cohorts were the Roman gods of the household. Before the influence of the Greek gods, Roman religion was relatively straight-forward and limited to the worship of spirits, each with its own sphere of domestic or farming influence. No mythology or stories attached to the spirits or *numina*, as they were called; they were not personified, they did not interact with one another, and no mythology grew up around them. Instead, each performed a specific function in his or her allotted area of responsibility. These were usually important events in life – birth, marriage and death – and in agriculture – harvesting, sowing and looking after the land. There were spirits to cover every eventuality, such as Sterculius, or Dunger, who looked after fertilising the land, or Vagitanus, Wailer, connected with a baby's birth. The *numina* did not have bodily forms, as the Greek gods were envisaged; instead they acted as the spirit or force of what they represented. These spirits were revered at their own little shrine in every Roman household and it was important to keep them sweet to ensure the family's continued good luck.

As well as the *numina* listed in the table on page 125 there were two other Roman gods, originally spirits of the household, who grew in stature and were

ROMAN HOUSEHOLD SPIRITS

Lares The Lar originally looked after the borders of a farm or land, and later became associated with boundaries, landmarks and neighbourhoods. Lares also looked after the whole household.

Penates The group of spirits who oversaw the household supplies and ensured that there was never want in the house.

Genius The guardian spirit of the family. Ultimately the genius came to be the guardian of places and even institutions, like the state.

Manes The spirits of the dead, especially the ancestral spirits in a family. A ceremony was held every year in honour of these ancestral ghosts to make sure they stayed contented in their place.

eventually personified to be included in the list of major deities.

Vesta The hearth goddess had originally started out as a household spirit but was later personified and given the stature of her Greek equivalent, Hestia. In the temple of Vesta in the Forum the goddess's sacred flame was tended and kept alight by the Vestal Virgins, priestesses of her cult chosen from the free – often noble – Roman families as children, to serve in the temple for 30 years. One particular Vestal, Rhea Silvia, played a central part in the founding of Rome (*see p. 130*). The Vestals also offered sacrifices and prayers for the state and rekindled the fire in the temple every March 1. The goddess also had her own feast day on June 9, Vestalia.

Janus The god who gave his name to January, first month of the new year, was the only major Roman god not to have a Greek equivalent. Wholly Roman, he presided over beginnings, openings and doorways. He looked backwards and forwards at the same time and so he was usually depicted with two faces – the origin of the old description of a duplicitous person, 'Janus-faced'.

Two-faced Janus pictured on a coin

Janus had originally been worshipped as a household deity. Those praying to the gods always mentioned him first, before any other god, in sacrifices and prayers and his blessing was invoked on the start of every day, month, year; on the sowing of crops; and the start of any important endeavour. Like Vesta, he was symbolically present in the Forum, at the heart of the Roman state. The Arch of Janus, his sacred gateway – with his statue looking in opposite directions at the same time – had its doors ceremonially opened when Rome was at war and stayed that way until the army came home.

Rome's Historical Myths

The rich culture and mythology of the Greeks obviously had a powerful influence on the Romans and they lifted whole chunks of it to embellish and fill in the gaps in their own history, so taking the old mythology off in a new direction and giving it a new slant. This new direction emphasised the Romans' search for an explanation of their place in the world – their interest was in historical myth rather than religious.

ROME'S FOUNDERS: THE TROJANS

The Greeks' destruction of Troy became an important event in Roman myth. Homer had written of Aeneas but his story was given full mythic power by the Roman poet Vergil in his *Aeneid*. Aeneas was a Trojan prince and military commander of divine descent who,

THE KEY DATES IN ROME BC

c.2000 BC The first settlers arrive in Italy from the north

c.900 BC The Etruscans arrive by sea; their origins are uncertain but they may have come from western Asia

753 BC The founding of the city of Rome; it was ruled by a succession of kings, some Etruscan

750 BC Greek settlers arrive in southern Italy and Sicily

510 BC The Roman Republic was founded

by 400 BC Rome was the dominant territory among the Latin alliance

338 BC Rome defeated its former Latin allies; the alliance was disbanded

by 264 BC Rome dominated the whole of Italy by either annexation or alliance

241 BC onwards Relentless expansion of Roman power and influence continued, beginning with Sicily and Sardinia, then moving further afield to Carthage, western Asia, Europe and Egypt

49 BC Julius Caesar takes power

27 BC Octavian becomes the first emperor, with the name Augustus; the Republic ended

VERGIL'S *AENEID*

Vergil wrote his *Aeneid*, the epic account of Aeneas's voyages, in the reign of Augustus, far removed from the action of the times he wrote of. His account was intended to aggrandise both Rome and Augustus, giving both distinguished origins.

by the design of the gods, had escaped the slaughter after Troy fell. Detailed were Aeneas's flight from Troy; his wanderings in the Mediterranean; his coming to Carthage and his love for Dido, the city's queen; her suicide on his departure to his destiny; and his landing, first in Sicily then in Italy after seven years' wandering. The Trojans eventually settled in peace in Latium, south of Rome, where Aeneas married the local king's daughter, Lavinia. The Trojans were to give up their name and language but the Latins would adopt some of the Trojans' rituals and worship. Aeneas's son Ascanius – also later given the name Iulus, emphasising his links to the Julian family of Julius Caesar – founded the city of Alba Longa; his family ruled as kings in the area for centuries; and Romulus and Remus, founders of Rome, were his descendents.

ROMULUS AND REMUS

Rhea Silvia was a descendant of Aeneas's at about four centuries' remove, a Vestal Virgin who became pregnant by the god Mars. Rhea's power-hungry uncle had deposed her father, Numitor, from the kingship of Alba Longa and when her children, twin boys, were born, he threw her into prison and set them adrift in a basket on the Tiber to die. But the basket was washed ashore where the boys were suckled by a wolf and fed by a woodpecker – both animals sacred to their divine father. A local shepherd found them and took them home to bring them up as his own.

Romulus and Remus with their wolf-mother

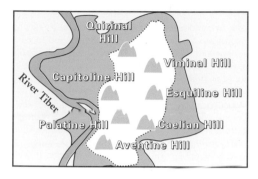

The seven hills on which the new city was built

The boys grew up strong and powerful enough to restore their grandfather to his kingship. But the restless pair also wanted a city of their own to rule. There are different versions to account for Romulus's ultimate domination of the new city, to be sited where they had been saved from death in their infancy; one of the most common is that there was disagreement over where it should be sited on the Palatine Hill. Remus, in a calculated insult, jumped over the foundation of the new city wall that Romulus and his men had painstakingly laid out and his twin, in a fit of anger, murdered him on the spot. The surviving twin named the city after himself.

THE RAPE OF THE SABINE WOMEN

Keen to build up the population, Romulus encouraged all comers to settle in Rome, and social outcasts and criminals of all types found a ready home there. The result was that the inhabitants of the new city were shunned by neighbouring tribes, who would not allow their daughters to marry Roman men. Without women Rome could hardly last beyond the present generation, so Romulus conceived a plan. He ordered a harvest festival to be held in Rome to which neighbouring tribes, including the Sabines, were invited. At the festival the Roman men attacked the Sabine men before abducting their daughters. Tribal war was the inevitable result but, surprisingly, the kidnapped women intervened between the warring tribes to plead that their husbands and fathers should not kill one another. (This Roman mythical event was the inspiration for the Hollywood musical, *Seven Brides for Seven Brothers*.)

Romulus ruled the new city for 40 years before vanishing without trace during a tornado on the Campus Martius (Mars Field, dedicated to his father). He was later worshipped as a god by the name of Quirinus and his feast-day was celebrated on March 13, Quirinalia.

The tradition of the deification of rulers was one that continued through Rome's history, with several of the city's leaders having divine associations; a spirit appeared to urge Julius Caesar to cross the Rubicon

and attack Rome, and a comet that appeared in 44 BC
was taken to be his newly-dead spirit reaching heaven.
The emperors themselves were believed to be gods on
earth and were worshipped while they were still alive.

THE SIBYLLINE BOOKS

Obsessed as they were with their own past, the
Romans were just as interested as the Greeks had
been in discovering what fate had in store in the
future. They had even more ways than the Greeks did
of trying to discover the future although their means
of discovering what fate held in store were slightly
different. One of the most important was a set of
three books written by a sibyl or ecstatic prophetess
who lived in a shrine at Cumae, near Naples. Sibyls
lived throughout the ancient world but this one had
particular significance to Rome.

She had a set of nine books containing prophecies of
Rome's future and offered to sell them at a huge price
to the early Roman king Tarquinius Priscus, Tarquin
the Old. When the king refused to buy them she
burnt three and offered him the remaining six at the
same price. He refused again, and watched her burn
three more books before being psyched into buying
the last three at the full price of the original set. The
books were regarded as sacred and were kept by a
special priesthood, only to be consulted on the orders
of the Senate in times of grave national emergency.

THE FUTURE OF ROME

Finally, one of the strongest of Roman historical myths still echoes down to the present day. It concerned the continued existence of Rome, the eternal city:

As long as the Colosseum stands,
Rome will stand.
When the Colosseum falls,
Rome too will fall.
When Rome falls,
The world will fall.

Later Religious Influences

Unlike the Greeks, or the insular Egyptians, Roman society was too active, dynamic and outward looking to be content with just one form of religion and mythology. The state religion, with its essentially passive involvement of the people and its failure to deliver what was asked of it, especially in hard times, made people look elsewhere for spiritual fulfilment. By the end of the Republic, many were already moving to other forms of worship which offered more than just passive observation and little else. These were some of the commonest:

- Mithraism: From the Middle East and India, this worship became a mystery cult popular among Roman soldiers and officers. Mithras was a Persian soldier-god of life, the sun and fertility as well as a mediator between earth and heaven. Mithras's cult promised life after death and stressed the equal worth of all men – although not women.

- Cult of Cybele: Cybele was a Western Asian mother-earth goddess who was also at the head of a mystery religion. This was a cult popular with women. Cybele's lover Attis castrated himself and bled to death but the emphasis of the Roman celebrations was on the cycle of the seasons and again with life after death. The initiation rites for Cybele's priests required them to castrate themselves.

- Cult of Isis: Worship of this Egyptian goddess (*see p. 34*) became popular when Cleopatra visited Rome in 45 BC. Isis's cult called for self-discipline and promised life after death.

- Judaism: After their 63 BC conquest of Palestine – later Judaea – the Romans were influenced by Judaism. But this religion's influence was not long-lasting: the Jews refused to worship the emperor as they were required, and would not settle under Roman rule. The Romans eventually destroyed Jerusalem's Great Temple in 70 AD.

- Christianity: Founded by the Jewish followers of Jesus in Judaea, Christianity was another religion stressing the worthiness of each individual and offering life after death. But with this one there was no need for initiation – its mysteries were available to all. Like the Jews, the Christians would not worship the emperor and were persecuted by the Romans. But the religion spread to such an extent that it was declared the state religion in 394 AD.

CELTIC MYTHOLOGY

The Celts

The mythology and legend of the ancient Celts has
played a major role in shaping the development of the
British Isles and beyond. But a degree of mystery
surrounds not just the mythology of the Celts, but
their very being. Theirs was an oral, not a written
society, and relatively little identifiable evidence
survives to give clues to their way of life.

ORIGINS

The diverse tribes now called Celts were Indo-
European, probably first emerging as an identifiable
'people' near the River Danube around 1000 BC. As
their population increased they began to expand their
territory into the surrounding areas of central Europe.
They were masters of diverse technologies – skilled in
working metal, building roads and weapons and in
farming. They were also ferocious warriors and as
such were feared even by the Romans, whose city they
overran around 290 BC. At the full extent of their
power in the second half of the last millennium BC
their lands stretched from Turkey in the east to
Ireland in the west (*see p. 138*).

Celtic culture spread outwards from its original base in central Europe

The arrival of the first Celts in Britain is thought to date from around 800 BC, expanding across England, Wales, Scotland and Ireland. Along with Gaul the British Isles are the main source of information about the Celts and their mythology.

SOURCES

Other than evidence uncovered by archeologists, there is little documented evidence of the Celtic way of life. Because they preferred to record their laws and traditions in songs, stories and poetry, it was not until after the Roman occupation of previously Celtic areas that any written records of their lives came to be kept. Other records were written by monks, who found the

THE IRISH SAGAS

The Irish mythological sagas are usually divided into four main groups, or cycles of stories.

- **The Mythological Cycle** relates tales of the Celtic spirits and gods
- **The Ulster Cycle** relates tales of the Irish heroic warrior aristocracy
- **The Historical Cycle** relates tales of 'actual' people of Celtic Ireland
- **The Fenian Cycle** relates tales of Fionn Mac Cumaill and his warriors, the Fianna

customs of the pagan Celts distasteful and often did not understand them; in both cases, those recording the Celts' lives and beliefs had little reason to

THE MABINOGION

Five of the 11 stories in this set of medieval Welsh tales are lifted from Welsh Celtic myth.

- **Pwyll pendefig Dyfed** Pwyll prince of Dyfed
- **Branwen ferch Llyr** Branwen daughter of Llyr
- **Manawydan fab Llyr** Manawydan son of Llyr
- **Math fab Mathonwy** Math son of Mathonwy
- **Culhwch & Olwen**

represent them fairly. But it was thanks to Christian monks that some of the most famous sets of sagas survived at all – the Irish and Welsh Sagas.

Celtic Mythology

CULTURAL INFLUENCES

As in most ancient societies, the natural world was the main influence on the way of life and beliefs. Celtic festivals were based around the changing seasons, and other aspects of the land around them helped shape their world-view. They regarded the earth as sacred, as the original source of all living things. The sun was the main life-giving force in their lives, and fire, as its representative, was central to many of their festivals and ceremonies. Their gods, too, were often spirits associated with the natural landscape – such as trees and rivers – rather than taking human form.

THE NATURAL WORLD

Water The life-giving properties of water are a basic and recurring theme in many belief systems. As part of their celebration of the Beltane festival (*see p. 156*), the druids (*see p. 149*) collected May dew to use in their rituals. Wells, rivers and lakes were all the dwelling places of supernatural creatures, and the route to the Other World after death was usually described as being across or through a body of water.

There are a number of tales of underwater cities in Celtic legend, and this may be the origin of the story of the lost city of Atlantis, a place of great wealth which was deluged with water as a punishment for the pride and excesses of its inhabitants. One legend stated that survivors of Atlantis colonised parts of Britain where they became the first druids. Breton legend has a very similar myth in the disappearing city of Ys.

Trees As part of their fundamental respect for all aspects of the natural world, trees were highly revered by the ancient Celts. Each one was thought to have its own spirit, like the Greek dryads – spirits of the tree. The oak, the most strong and ancient, was foremost among the trees, and is particularly associated with the druids, who were often buried in the hollowed trunk of an oak tree. Oak was used for fires at solstice festivals and Beltane rites, and was considered particularly special as it was where mistletoe was to be found.

Elder, rowan, birch and hazel were also important trees. Hazelnuts were a source of creativity and fertility, giving the gift of prophecy to druids and knowledge and musical ability to bards, and hazel was the wood of the water-diviner's rod.

Mistletoe The parasitic mistletoe shrub is very much associated with oak on which it grows. Even today, it is still most often associated with the druids, who harvested it with a golden sickle and used it in unrecorded sacred ceremonies. Of course, the plant's main significance today is in the Christmas practice of kissing under the mistletoe – a practice probably dating back to a druidic fertility rite.

Animals The Celts had a strong affinity with animals – the druids, for example, were thought able not just to be able to communicate with them, but even to shape-shift, transforming themselves into animals. Animals were also used in important ceremonials: according to an Irish tradition, when the king died, the royal druids would assemble and sacrifice an ox. The animal's flesh was made into a broth which they ate before spending the night sleeping on its skin. Their subsequent dreams would reveal the identity of the future king.

But the animal most associated with the Celts was the horse. Horses were very important animals in Celtic life – they were represented on coins and artefacts, and their carefully buried remains have been identified among archeological discoveries. They provided a means of transport and sport and gave advantage in battle, as well as easing the burden of load-bearing work. Goddesses associated with the horse often took on its form, giving rise to tales of magical horses, who turn into beautiful women when they are caught. The deity Epona (*see p. 161*) was a horse-goddess. The ancient chalk horse figure carved into the hillside at Uffington in Berkshire celebrates the cultural importance of the horse.

Deer, too, were common in Celtic mythology, often appearing as other-worldly messengers. Many hunters came across them in the form of the sacred White Doe or White Stag. Cernunnos, the god of all living creatures, was depicted as a man with a stag's horns (*see p. 160*). Horned human figures, such as Herne the Hunter, also recur in legends throughout Celtic areas (*see p. 162*).

Unlike the owl in other traditions, the oldest and wisest creature in Celtic mythology was the salmon. The fish gained wisdom after eating magic hazelnuts which fell from the tree hanging over its home.

Birds Crows and ravens were associated particularly

Raven

with battle. The battle goddess, the Morrighan, often took the form of a raven. The significance of raven-legend in Britain continues to this day. According to legend, the ravens at the Tower of London keep the country free of invasion, and their departure would mean disaster. However, the fact that their wings are kept clipped means they can't go anywhere, even if they wanted to!

DEATH AND THE OTHER WORLD

Central to the Celtic religion was a belief in a life after death, a belief that astounded – and ultimately, was to influence the beliefs of – the Romans who came into contact with them.

The Celtic Other World was the realm of the dead which existed alongside or even within the mortal world. It was possible to accidentally stumble into it – hunters following a white stag or boar might find themselves there, having actually followed a spirit. Taking a particular path at a fork in the road or crossing an unfamiliar bridge were other ways in. This was also the way into the paradise of the Celtic spirits

The boar: another mystical animal for the Celts

known as 'Tir na n'Og', the Land of Youth. Like visitors to other mythological enchanted lands, those who wandered in spent a few blissful hours there before returning to the mortal world, only to discover that they had actually been gone for many years.

The Celts believed that immediately after a person's death, their soul needed a physically clear passage to make its way into the Other World. Rituals around this belief included opening doors, windows and locks and laying seriously ill people on the floor. These pagan practices were still found in remoter parts of Scotland long after the Reformation in the 16th century.

As in many ancient cultures, the most respected warriors of Celtic tribes were buried complete with weapons and battle chariots. Their horses were also

A dolmen – believed to be a Celtic burial-place

slaughtered for burial alongside them, ensuring that even in the Other World they were always battle-ready. This may be connected to the Celts' belief in a form of reincarnation, where their greatest heroes were only asleep, waiting in a state of readiness in case they were required to save the nation in a time of peril. This belief lingered on into the Christian era, with Britain's greatest hero, Arthur, believed to be sleeping and awaiting his call to go out and save his country.

It was in the Other World that the gods came together to decide the fate of mortals. This might be done by a game, particularly in deciding the outcome of a battle: a chess-like game would be played, with the winner deciding the destiny of those on the battle-field. The gods also had the power to summon those who had displeased them, and set them a series of tasks. These share a common theme with other legends where a hero has transgressed and must prove himself – most obviously the Twelve Labours of Heracles (see p. 100)

Celtic Religious Practice

Some of the rites associated today with Celtic religion and mythology are gruesome. Sacrifices were frequently made to appease or to pay tribute to the gods, and sometimes the victims in the rituals have been human. If these live human sacrifices did take place, the victims may well have been condemned criminals. This practice is not overtly stated in the existing records, but it is implicit in some ceremonies held by the druids around Samhain, the winter feast which was traditionally a time of fire festivals (see p. 156). Large wicker figures were erected, the victims (animal or human) were put inside, then the whole structure was set alight. Archeological investigations of animal remains found at Avebury and Stonehenge seem to bear this out.

As well as the sacred Samhain fires, another druidic sacrifice ritual was the 'triple death'. (Three was a sacred Celtic number.) Hanging or strangulation was followed by stabbing or burning, then lastly immersion in water. There is even an account of Arthur's magician Merlin being killed in a variant on this method, where he is stabbed, stoned and drowned.

Religious practice spilled over into everyday life, of course. Hunters had a set of practices to appease the spirits of their prey. A number of rituals developed, such as taking the bones of the slaughtered animal back to where it had been killed, and leaving them to be repossessed by its spirit.

Human heads were of particular importance to the Celts, although their actual significance is not fully understood. They were depicted in Celtic art, particularly stonework, and featured in religious practice. After victory in combat, the victor would sever the head of his enemy and keep it as a trophy. The grisly remains of slain enemies were preserved or used as decoration around the entrance to the house as evidence of military prowess; there may also have been a deeper religious significance.

Decapitation is a frequent occurrence in Celtic legend. The story of Sir Gawaine and the Green Knight – although dating from the 14th century – is typical. The Green Knight arrives at the court of King Arthur in the dead of winter and challenges the knights to cut off his head, on condition he can do the same to them in a year's time. Only Gawaine accepts the challenge and cuts off the knight's head. When he sets off twelve months later to keep his end of the bargain, his life is spared because he has proved himself worthy.

The story of the Ulster warrior CuChulainn is an Irish version. He too accepted a stranger's challenge to cut off his head, only to see the mysterious knight clamber immediately to his feet and demand a return blow. CuChulainn knelt and bowed his head without hesitation; his bravery earned him his life. Such challenges always took place in the depths of winter, with the Green Knight representing the old spirit of the forest, challenged by one symbolising the strength and vigour of the new year ahead.

DRUIDS AND BARDS

DRUIDS

To many people, the defining image of Celtic society is the druid. The white-robed figures that still converge on Stonehenge every summer for the solstice see themselves as direct descendants of the druidic tradition. It is likely that the word 'druid' originates from *duir*, or 'oak', the tree they held in greatest esteem (*see p. 141*).

The Celts venerated their druids, guardians of their religion and law and royal spiritual advisors; they were mystics, prophets and healers. Although the druids are not described in any of the sources as a priesthood, this is almost certainly the role they played in ancient Celtic society. They were responsible for regulating religious practices, such as making live sacrifices to the gods (*see p. 147*).

A large part of the druids' continuing appeal is that so little is known about them. Everything they learned in their many years of training had to be committed to memory, including laws, festivals, the genealogies of their tribes and more. Controlling the flow of information meant their knowledge and powers remained inaccessible, so increasing their own indispensability.

One certainty is that theirs was not an easy career option – our fanciful modern image of a group of ascetic, long-bearded, white-gowned tree-huggers is a total fiction. Druids were required to be extremely tough. Hirtius' *Conquest of Gaul*, written around the time of Julius Caesar, helped shed some light on the druids and their practices. It suggests druids underwent a gruelling training period which lasted around 20 years, and Caesar himself is said to have noted that British druids were the most respected of all, teaching the finest students of the druidic arts.

BARDS

While not given the same high esteem as druids, bards were also respected figures who kept alive their tribe's traditions. Their main role was to provide in story and song their versions of key tribal events; they usually accompanied themselves on the harp. And during battles the warring tribes' bards kept well away from the fighting, recording the exploits of the warriors.

Bards were usually very well rewarded for their work. According to legend, they could ask for anything they wanted in return for their music – a perk open to exploitation. The magician Gwydian pretended to be a bard to trick his way into the court of Pryderi, king of Dyfed, whose swine he coveted. Following his performance, the king asked him to chose his reward, and Gwydian chose the swine. One of the most famous Welsh bards, the poet Myrddin, may have been the basis for King Arthur's seer and advisor, Merlin.

ARTEFACTS

Archaeological discoveries at Celtic sites suggest theirs was a relatively sophisticated society, with developed aesthetic taste. There were strong traditions of art and craftsmanship, including fine jewellery such as the famous Celtic neck torcs (worn by the god Cernunnos in the picture on p. 160). But not all the Celts' crafts were purely decorative. Their warrior-aristocracy wore finely crafted shields, swords and helmets.

HALLOWS

Among the most important artefacts in Celtic legend were the Hallows, the Celtic kingly regalia or emblems of empowerment. The Hallows of Ireland are listed below, and the Thirteen Treasures of Britain, found in Welsh sources and said to have been guarded by the magician Merlin, are very similar (*see p. 153*).

The common feature of these artefacts is that they work only for those worthy of them. Their magical powers are effective for the brave and pious – in the hands of

---

THE HALLOWS OF IRELAND

The Stone of Fal place of inauguration for the Irish kings

The Spear of Lugh gave victory in every battle

The Sword of Nuadu none could escape unwounded from it

The Cauldron of Dagda no one would leave the cauldron unsatisfied

THE 13 TREASURES OF BRITAIN

1 Dyrnwyn, sword of Rhydderch the Generous, a magical sword like Arthur's Excalibur.

2 The Hamper of Gwyddno Garanhir – if food for one was put in, food for a hundred came out.

3 The Horn of Bran dispensed whatever drink was wanted, like the Grail.

4 The Chariot of Morgan the Wealthy. It took its owner wherever he wished to go.

5 The Halter of Clyno Eiddyn, which would bring the owner any horse he wanted.

6 The Knife of Llawfronedd the Horseman, which could carve for 24 men.

7 The Cauldron of Diwrnach the Giant – it would not heat a coward's food, only a brave man's.

8 The Whetstone of Tudwal Tudglyd. If a brave man used it to sharpen his sword, anyone wounded by the weapon would die.

9 The Coat of Padarn Red-coat, which only fitted a nobleman.

10 and 11 The Crock and Dish of Rhygenydd, which contained the owner's favourite food.

12 The Chessboard of Gwenddolau – the pieces played the game themselves.

13 The Mantle of Arthur, a cloak of invisibility.

a coward, they are useless. Ownership of these symbols of regal power was therefore convincing evidence of the holder's right to rule, a belief which continued for hundreds of years – from the legend of Arthur demonstrating his royal blood by being the only one able to pull the sword from the stone, to the close-guarding of the monarch's regalia, their symbols of office.

CAULDRON

A recurring motif in Celtic mythological stories is the cauldron, which can be used as a force for either good or evil. It played a part in everyday life as the main cooking utensil in the home, but legendary cauldrons were also believed to be capable of dispensing life, death, creativity and wisdom. Magical cauldrons were used by the druids to produce potions and other concoctions. And a cauldron featured in one of the Thirteen Treasures of Britain: the Cauldron of Diwrnach would boil the meat of the brave instantly, but would not cook the food of a coward.

SACRED SITES

Stone circles and henges are features of the landscape in many parts of Britain. They have long been popularly associated with the druids – most famously the ancient stone circle of Stonehenge on Salisbury Plain in Wiltshire. But although Stonehenge and others like Avebury were almost certainly sites of

The most famous of Britain's pre-Christian sites, Stonehenge was long associated with the Celts

pagan worship and possibly of astronomical significance, they pre-date the arrival of the Celts by hundreds of years, with most having been constructed between 2500 and 1500 BC. As the Christians later did with some Celtic beliefs, it is more likely that the druids adapted pre-existing religious sites and practices to expand their own influence in the lands where they settled.

FESTIVALS

There were several key festivals in the Celtic calendar, based, like so much in their mythology, around a natural progression – this time, of the seasons.

Samhain This was the Celtic New Year festival, which occurred around 31 October and 1 November, when we now celebrate Hallowe'en and the Christian festival of the Eve of All Hallows, and All Hallows or All Saints Day. Bonfires were lit all over the country to remember the sun and encourage its return. This was the time of the dead and the beginning of the rule of the Cailleach Bheur (see p. 160).

Beltane This was the mid-point of the year, at May Day, and one of the most important times of the Celtic year. On Beltane day (1st May) all domestic fires were put out and local people would gather around the hilltop, where bonfires were lit at sunset and watched till dawn. The embers were then taken home by those attending and used to light their fires at home, which would not be completely extinguished until the next Beltane evening.

Imbolc/Oimelc On the first day of February, Imbolc coincided with the start of the lambing season. This is the closest to our festival of Easter, which borrows its egg-rolling from the Celts, for whom in turn the egg was a sign of the approach of spring and the appearance of new life from apparent barrenness. The

A potent symbol, past and present – the Yule log

festival is associated with Brigit (*see p. 159*), the representative of spring.

Ligmasad The time of the August harvest, this was a time of celebration and thanksgiving.

Yule The Yule festival took place around the winter solstice, and was a time of celebration to lighten the dark nights of winter. It centred around the Celtic worship of the sun, aiming to persuade it to return. The Yule celebration was just one of the festivals taken over by the Christian church, and the origins of some of our still-practised Christmas traditions may lie in the Celtic festivities: the Yule log refers back to the ancient communal Yule bonfire; and kissing under the mistletoe probably began as a druidic fertility rite. Decorative holly and ivy signifies a reverence for trees, especially evergreens – manifest now in our Christmas trees – which were a symbol and promise of new life and growth, even in the depths of cold winter.

Celtic Gods

Unravelling the names and identities of the Celtic gods is no easy job. There are literally hundreds of different names from the various areas where the Celts settled, with different spellings in the Irish, Welsh, British and Breton traditions just adding to the confusion. This complex situation is not helped by the reluctance of the ancient Celts to use their gods' names at all, in case the names were used by their enemies to invoke the power of their own gods against them. 'I swear by the gods by whom my people swear' is a recurring oath, or else the gods are referred to by anonymous titles such as 'The Mighty One'.

Andraste   The warrior goddess worshipped by British heroine and warrior queen Boudicca (d. 62 AD); many sacred groves were dedicated to Andraste.

Angus mac Og   Irish god of youth and son of Dagda (*see p. 161*). Conceived in the morning and born by evening, his enchanted birth gave him power over time.

Anu/Dana/Danu   Goddess of fertility and prosperity. Mother of the gods, she represents mother earth.

Badb/Badhbh   The goddess of life, war and wisdom, she is associated with the sacred symbol of the cauldron (*see p. 154*), and with ravens (*see p. 144*), whose form she could also assume. She is one of the three manifestations of the Morrighan (*see p. 162*), the archetypal female deity.

Banshee   A harbinger of death, this female spirit would wail outside the home of those about to die. She is associated with the Washer at the Ford (*see p. 163*), one of the three personalities of the Morrighan (*see p. 162*).

Belatucadros   The horned god of the north, his name means 'fair shining one' and the Romans associated him with Mars.

Belinus/Bel   The powerful lord of life and death. Belinus was the god of the sun, fire and fertility. He was venerated by the druids and their Beltane fires were lit to mark his feast (The name 'Beltane' means 'Fire of Bel').

Brigit/Brid   Although she became subsumed in the cult of the Christian St Brigit, Brigit was originally the goddess of wisdom and fertility. She is most associated with the spring festival of Imbolc, when she successfully challenges and sees off the hag of winter. Brigid was also known as Brigantia in northern Britain, and the Romans saw her as a manifestation of Minerva.

Cailleach Bheur/Cailleach Bheare   The blue-faced hag who represented winter and controlled both the weather and the seasons. She was reborn every year at Samhain, the festival which fell on 31 October, and ruled until 1 February. The hag or *cailleach* is a widespread figure in Celtic literature, often portrayed as the personification of the land, holding the gift of kingship. She appears as a hideous hag to the potential king and asks him to kiss her; if he accepts, he has proved himself worthy, having shown his acceptance of all, and the Loathly Lady – as the hag was often known – is transformed into a fair maiden.

Cathubodua The Celtic goddess of war, her name means 'battle crow' and she is the equivalent of the Irish Badh.

Cernunnos Depicted with the antlers of a stag, his name means 'Horned One' – he was the lord of the animals and living things. (The torcs he wears on his neck and holds in his hand demonstrate his kingship.)

Cernunnos

Cerridwen/Caridwen Goddess of nature, she is keeper of the cauldron in Wales and is associated with Brigit.

Dagda Father of the gods, he was the chief god of the druids and the Irish Celts. He was the son of Belinus and Danu, and mated with the Morrighan over a river. He was also known as 'The Great Father' and 'The One of Great Knowledge'. Dagda had three attributes:

- a magic harp that could produce music for sleep, music for laughter and music for woe;

- a pot or cauldron from which no-one went away hungry;

- and a magic club, similar to the hammer of Thor. one end killed and the other revived the dead.

Don/Donn Living on one of the islands off the Irish coast, he was god of the land of the dead and guarded the entrance to the Other World. He controlled the elements and could send storms to wreck ships.

Epona Goddess of horsemen and animals, she also looked after the harvest. She was often depicted seated semi-naked on a horse or with a horse's head, and has been identified with the Welsh Rhiannon.

Finn mac Cool/Fionn mac Cumhal/Fingal Although not strictly a god, he had godlike properties. Raised by a druidess, he was both wise prophet and fierce warrior. His acquired wisdom came after burning his thumb while cooking the salmon of knowledge – he sucked his thumb and the gift of knowledge was his. He went on to become head of the Fianna/Fenians, the warband of 150 of the most powerful Irish chiefs and druids. Like many of the heroic figures of his time, he is said to be sleeping in the Other World, awaiting the day of his return.

Goibhniu/Gofannon Known for his therapeutic powers, he was the god of blacksmiths and craftsmen.

Herne the Hunter A legendary horned spirit, he conducted the dead into the Other World. Herne is said to have led the wild hunt, where the spectral leader and his men, accompanied by baying hounds, rode through the air and over the hills. Known as Herne in southern England, in Wales he was Gwynn ap Nudd, with other names in other areas.

Mab/Maeve The queen of the Other World.

Manannan mac Lir God of commerce and the sea, his name literally means 'Son of the Sea'. He often took the form of a heron, especially for his night visits to mortal women.

Morrighan The Great Queen in Irish myth, she is the archetypal form of the goddess. She could appear as one of three entities: Macha, the goddess of fertility; Badb, the goddess of water and the Washer at the Ford; and Neman, the goddess of battle. She is particularly associated with war, and normally took the form of a battle crow or raven.

Mother Goddess   Generic mother goddess figures who represented the earth were very important in Celtic worship and are often depicted bearing the fruits of the earth – loaves, fruit, beer etc. They were the guardians of the earth, of land and plenty.

Nimue/Niniane/Viviene   Spirit from the Other World who persuaded Merlin to reveal the secrets of his magic which she then used against him to trap him inside the trunk of a tree.

Nuada/Nodens/Nudd   The god of waters and the sea, he became associated with Neptune. He was also known as 'Nuadha of the Silver Hand' after he lost his hand in battle and had a replacement cast from silver.

Ogma/Ogmios   Son of the Dagda and brother of Brigit, he was god of eloquence and poetry.

Rosmerta   A Celtic goddess whose name translates as 'good purveyor'.

Scathach/Scota   The patroness of blacksmiths and prophecy, she is said to have trained the famous Celtic warrior CuChulainn and prophesied his success. The island of Skye in Scotland takes its name from hers.

Sulis   Goddess of the Other World, knowledge and prophesy.

Washer at the Ford   One of the manifestations of the Morrighan, this spirit would appear to those about to die, washing out blood-stained clothes.

NORSE MYTHOLOGY
The Norsemen

The traditional image of the fearsome Viking – horned-helmeted, bearded pillager, rapist and merciless killer rampaging unchecked across Europe – has been the popular perception of the ancient Norse people for hundreds of years. But these ferocious hordes only appeared in the 9th and 10th centuries: hundreds of years into the development of Norse society and the growth of Scandinavian belief and mythology.

ORIGINS

The Norse peoples, of Indo-European stock, inhabited areas that are now north Germany and Scandinavia. The earliest recognisable roots of Norse mythology are in the Scandinavian Bronze Age, from around 1600–450 BC: archeological discoveries of fine metal and stoneworks from this early period show primitive figures of gods and goddesses.

From the 3rd to the 6th centuries AD, there was great upheaval in the Roman Empire and across western Europe. As the Empire split and ingressions were made by other tribes, whole groups of people migrated from one part of the continent to another. The Northern tribes moved into what is now Denmark and Sweden.

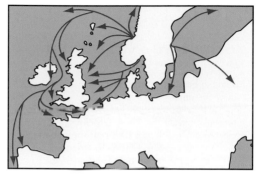

Norse migration out from Scandinavia

At the same time, the cult of Odin (or Wodan, as he was also known) began to flourish in the North.

But these Scandinavians were to move a great deal further afield over the centuries. By the 10th century, the Vikings dominated the shores of Britain and Ireland, had settled in Normandy and ventured even as far afield as Greenland – one school of thought believes they were the first modern settlers of America, pre-dating Columbus by centuries. Such a wide scattering meant diversity of belief inevitably crept in to different areas. Other than the main gods, whose cults seem to have been widespread, which gods were favoured depended on local circumstances.

SOURCES

Like other pagan societies, the Northern peoples had no written tradition, passing on their laws, mythology and stories orally, through songs and verse. The only contemporary Scandinavian sources are runes – hieroglyphic symbols carved on wood, stone and metal – but these are very short, cryptic and hard to interpret.

Viking poets, or 'skalds', had a similar role to the Celtic bards: they were the guardians of the people's history and tradition. As such, they were held in very high esteem in their communities, and were welcomed with hospitality wherever they went. They embroidered rich stories of gods and heroes. Many Skaldic tales were not written down subsequently.

Some Latin and Greek writers, such as the Roman historian Tacitus (writing around 1 AD), recorded the development of Odin's cult. But the main sources of information about the beliefs and practices of the Norse people are the works known as the *Elder* or *Poetic Edda* and the *Prose Edda*. The *Poetic Edda* brings together poems relating ancient tales of the gods, culminating in the final battle of Ragnarok (*see p. 180*). These myths seem to come from a variety of locations and times, from the pre-Viking era to the time of the conversion of Iceland in 1000 AD.

Another poem telling the exploits of Scandinavian heroes is the Anglo-Saxon epic *Beowulf*. Despite its

PROSE EDDA

Snorri Sturlson was a poet, historian and politician writing in his native Icelandic around 1220. His *Prose Edda* (also known as the *Codex Regius*) was meant as a poets' handbook, to encourage ancient traditions and the custom of recording in verse.

The book gives instructions in the traditional constructions and themes of skaldic verse, as the legendary poems were known. It was written two centuries after Iceland converted to Christianity, so some have doubted his interpretation of the myths.

obvious Christian influences, it gives an insight into Scandinavian mythology, with elaborate tales of fearless heroes struggling against terrible mythic creatures.

Cultural Influences

CLIMATE AND COMMUNITY

The Northern peoples lived in small warrior tribes under an aristocratic leader. At times he would lead them away from their homes in search of new lands to settle. Their family unit and local community were of great importance to them – ties of blood and friendship were certainties in what was a nomadic and uncertain way of life. The main occupations open to

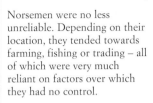

Norsemen were no less unreliable. Depending on their location, they tended towards farming, fishing or trading – all of which were very much reliant on factors over which they had no control.

Norse life was harsh, with everything subject to the vagaries of the changeable, inhospitable weather. All this was reflected in their myths , which sought ways to explain the world around them. Everything was attributed to the gods: the sound of thunder was Thor throwing his great hammer; the glaciers' cracking was the noise of frost giants; a rainbow was a bridge between the lands of mortals and gods. Different groups in society worshipped different gods: so fishermen honoured sea gods, while farmers paid homage to land and fertility deities.

Icebergs were believed to be home to the frost giants

Likewise the early cult of the sky god and earth goddess was based on the journey of the sun across the sky (an interpretation shared by almost every other pagan religion) and the changing seasons. The gods also made time pass, sending Night and Day driving their swift chariots through the sky. In another version, the sun and moon are chased back and forth across the sky by monstrous wolves.

Mythology and Belief

THE NATURAL WORLD

The natural world played a very important part in Norse mythology, from the creation stories to the end of the world at Ragnarok. No theme recurs more often than the tree, which is central to Norse mythology.

YGGDRASIL

At the earth's centre earth was the World Tree, most likely an ash, whose roots linked all the nine worlds ranged down it (see p. 179). It represented a joining of the realms of mortals, the dead and the gods. On top of the tree perched an eagle, a symbol of Odin; at its base was the spring of Mimir, source of wisdom, and coiled around its roots was a great serpent.

It was from Mimir's spring Odin wanted to drink so badly that he was prepared to exchange one of his

eyes in return. After drinking, Odin received the wisdom he sought. Another story relates that after receiving the wisdom Odin hung on the world tree for nine days and nights, pierced with a spear as a symbolic sacrifice to himself, just as sacrificial victims to him were speared and hung on a tree. But the magical runic alphabet was also on the tree, and Odin was able to take it, so gaining knowledge and power over death itself.

WATER

Norse legends show great respect for the sea, which was recognised as a force of destruction: below its waves lay the serpent who would ultimately overwhelm the earth. At the same time, it

To the Norse, the sea was the most potent of natural elements, bringing both life and death

was the source of life, providing water and food. Sailors and fishermen were particularly devoted to the god and goddess of the ocean, Aegir and his wife Ran (*see p. 184*).

ANIMALS AND PLANTS

The most commonly occurring animal in the legends is the wolf. Its role is ambivalent: on the one hand, it is the bringer of victory, and Odin was depicted with two wolves beside him in Valhalla. But the fearsome Fenrir, one of the monsters created by Loki (*see p. 186*), was also a wolf who overcame Odin and helped bring about the fall of the gods at Ragnarok. Fenrir was huge and ferocious, so the gods had decided that they should ask the dwarves to make a magical unbreakable rope to bind him. The wolf was suspicious when the gods suggested that they would bind him with the rope as a test of strength, and refused unless one of the gods would put an arm in his mouth as a guarantee that he would be able to escape. Only the brave Tyr agreed and, when the wolf discovered his bonds were unbreakable, bit the god's hand off at the wrist.

Birds Eagles and ravens were symbols and forms of Odin. As a bird, he could travel high and fast, looking down onto all the nine worlds. The eagle was the bird which perched on top of Yggdrasil, while ravens were linked with the Valkyries and death on the battlefield.

Boar The animal most associated with Freyr was the boar – specifically a golden boar called Gullinbursti, 'Goldbristles'. He could outrun any steed, and the golden bristles of his mane lit up the night. The boar symbol appears on weapons and shields: Freyr and the animal associated with him gave protection to their favoured warriors in battle. The boar represented fertility and the harvest, and was sacrificed to Freyr, Freya and Odin. The centrepiece of the meal at the feast in Valhalla was the magic boar, Saehrimnir, who was eaten every night only to revive to be hunted and eaten again the next day. Likewise, in the mortal world, a boar's head was often central to a banquet.

Horse The horse was very important in Scandinavian society. It carried the warrior into battle, and the horses of the battle-slainwere often buried with them to let the mounted battle continue in the afterlife. Horses were also sacrificed to the gods – the head and feet were preserved with the skin but everything else was eaten at the sacrificial feast which was to ensure prosperity and good seasons. In the Icelandic tradition, horses dedicated to Freyr could be ridden by no-one else, under pain of death.

Serpent The world serpent was coiled around the base of the world tree in the depths of the sea awaiting Ragnarok, when he would meet his greatest foe – Thor. The myth of the dragon or serpent is widespread of all myths, appearing in the legends of all nations.

Mistletoe Although mistletoe is most commonly associated with Celtic mythology, it also plays a small but vital role in Norse legends, in the story of the death of Balder. Balder was loved by his father Odin, so much that Frigg had asked all the plants and metals to vow not to hurt him, making him impervious to harm. But there was always an exception – in this case, mistletoe – so small Frigg forgot it. Troublesome Loki realised this and made a dart of mistletoe for Balder's brother Hodor to throw at Balder as a joke. The dart pierced his brother's heart and killed him. At the funeral, attended by all the gods, Hel agreed to a request to free Balder from the underworld, on condition that all things on earth wept for his loss. This they did, as the winter frosts and snows melt and weep each spring. But Loki transformed himself into an old woman and refused to weep for Balder, condemning him to spend eternity in the underworld. The fate of Balder, called the Good and the Beautiful, showed what inevitably befel these qualities on earth.

This story well shows the limits of the Norse gods' powers, with Odin unable to save his son from death. Odin's failure is linked to his final fall at Ragnarok.

Apples In common with many other mythologies, the apple was seen as a symbol of life and youth. The golden apples of eternal youth prevented the gods from ageing, and were guarded by the goddess Idun.

DEATH AND THE OTHER WORLD

In the Norse tradition, there were various ways of dealing with the body after death. One of these was the ship burial. Ships were a vital part of life for the sea-faring Scandinavians – their adventurers and fishermen relied on them for their lives. And just as fallen warriors were often buried with their horses, so those who lived on the sea might be buried with their ship. There is a famous 7th century example of this at Sutton Hoo in Suffolk, which shows a mixture of heathen and Christian traditions.

Ships were used for the burials of both men and women; they were offerings to the gods and

The spectacular end to Shetland's Up-helly-aa festival

played a part in processions. The burning boat is one of the most lasting images associated with Scandinavian lore, and the traditional burial for the great and the good is still commemorated in festivals in many places, including Shetland and York, areas where the Vikings were dominant for centuries. Funeral pyres were another method of sending Scandinavian society's high-born on their way to the next world.

Norse death traditions were often reminiscent of other mythologies, too. 'Banquets' seem to have been placed in the graves of the wealthy, echoing the legendary feasting in the hall of Valhalla. Other grave goods might include amulets of the gods with whom the person was most closely identified, and their animals. Warriors were buried with their spears and weapons, while small model spears were often buried with young boys who had died, possibly as a tribute to Odin.

Valhalla Norse warriors were expected to meet death on the battlefield bravely, if not gladly. They had to endure torture and death without complaint and bear no grudge into the afterlife. As their reward for courage, they spent the afterlife in Valhalla, the domain of Odin. Warriors who had died a heroic death were welcomed into his hall, where they feasted on boar flesh and drank mead every night, arising the next morning to do battle all day before the feasting began again in the

A modern-day depiction of Viking warrior

evening. The warriors in Valhalla were known as the Einheriar, and would come again to fight alongside Odin and the gods in the final battle at Ragnarok.

The Other World The land of the dead was ruled by Loki's daughter, the goddess Hel. The place itself, also sometimes called Hel, was in the realm of Niflheim. The way lay across the Echoing Bridge, which made a different sound according to who was crossing, and the entrance was guarded by Garm, a monstrous dog. It is not clear if the goddess took her name from the place, or vice versa.

ARTEFACTS

Bronze Age evidence suggests the dead were placed in burial mounds; warriors with their weapons and finely crafted pieces of jewellery and ornaments alongside high-born women. Two small bronze figures with axes in their hands and horned helmets on their heads were also uncovered in archeological digs – these were probably early representations of the gods.

Many bodies were buried with grave goods (*see p. 175*) and these often included amulets. As well as being buried with the dead, these symbols of the gods could be worn by the living and used to decorate the home. Small spears signified devotion to Odin, while hammers indicated followers of Thor. The symbol of Thor's hammer, Mjollnir, was frequently carved on memorial stones and worn around the neck. In the 10th century, thousands of small hammers were made in Scandinavia, in iron, bronze and even silver, for the god's better-off adherents. (By Christian times, the hammer shape subtly changed into a cross-shape.)

These artefacts were important in Norse legend. Mjollnir was made by dwarf-craftsmen and was a precious and powerful weapon. Jealous of the might of the Aesir gods, the giant Thrym stole the hammer and refused to give it back unless the goddess Freya was sent to be his wife. Disguising themselves as Freya and her handmaid, Thor and Loki went instead. After feasting, preparation for the wedding began and the hammer was laid in the lap of the 'bride' as a wedding gift. Thor and Loki immediately threw off their disguise, slew the giant and all the wedding guests, and returned to Asgard in triumph.

BELIEFS

Creation In the beginning there was only chaos, the emptiness known as Ginnungagap. Down the ages, a glow appeared in the south, which gradually become Muspell, the land of fire, lethal to all except those who lived there. Its guardian, Surt, was armed with a flaming sword which he would use to consume the earth with fire at the time of Ragnarok (see p. 180). In the north was Niflheim, the realm of ice and darkness. At its heart was the spring Hvergelmir from which flowed Elivagar, the twelve great rivers of Niflheim. As they flowed, they became colder and began to freeze. Where the heat of the south and the frozen wastes of the north met in the middle, they resulted in the great giant Ymir. Alongside him, there came a giant cow, which licked the salty blocks of ice to reveal Buri, the first god, encased in the ice. Ymir produced the first man and woman and the race of frost giants. He was slain by three gods, the sons of Bor (grandsons of Buri), who created the world from his remains. The earth was made from his flesh, the mountains from his bones, the cliffs from his teeth, his blood was spilled to form the oceans, and his skull formed the sky.

It was not just the world of mortals that was created at

THE NINE WORLDS OF NORSE MYTHOLOGY

Asgard The land of the gods of the Aesir, it was situated in splendour at the top of the tree

Vanaheim Realm of the Vanir gods

Alfheim The realm of the light elves, helpers of humans

In the middle levels of the great tree were:

Svartalheim Land of the dark elves, who made mischief against humans

Nidavellir The land of dwarves

Midgard The middle world, which was the realm of mortals

Jotunheim The frozen land of the frost giants

Muspell The southern land of fire, guarded by Surt with his flaming sword

And situated at the bottom of Yggdrasil:

Niflheim The land of darkness, ice and shadow, which included the world of the dead, the realm of Hel

this time. In total, there were nine worlds in Norse mythology, ranged all the way down the trunk of the great world tree, Yggdrasil (*see p. 169*). The tree connected the realms of gods, mortals, giants and the other supernatural beings of Scandinavian legend.

Ragnarok The basis for the Ragnarok legends is the Icelandic poem *Völuspá*, said to have been inspired by a volcanic eruption. It describes the final great battle between good and evil, leading to the destruction of the earth but followed by the rebirth of life. It showed the Viking view of life as a constant survival-battle between the forces of creation and those of destruction and chaos. Order was constantly threatened by floods, volcanic eruptions, snow and cold – metaphors not just for a perilous northern existence but for the internal battle waging in every individual.

According to the legend, after a great war and a severe winter lasting many years, the world serpent would emerge from the waters and bring a great flood bearing a ship made from the uncut nails of the dead. Surt leads the way out of Muspell as the wolf Fenrir and Hel's dog, Garm, break their bonds and go in search of the enemies who captured them. The gods are alerted by the horn of Heimdall but as Odin leads out his champions he is overcome and killed by his ancient enemy, Fenrir the wolf. Thor slays his foe the serpent but as it dies, he too is killed, by the poison spewing from its mouth. All that remains in the end is the world tree and two beings, Lif and Lifthrasir, who are destined to re-people the earth when it rises from the sea, cleansed of war and discord as it was in the first days of creation. It is the end of the old warring order, as the worlds of gods and mortals are overcome by catastrophic forces beyond their control, showing the vulnerability of the mortal world and punishing humans and gods for their mistakes.

PRACTICES

Sacrifice and Ceremony Sacrificial offerings played a major part in the worship of the Norse gods. These offerings could be either human or animal. Kings and warriors pledged to sacrifice the battle-slain to Odin in return for victory, with horses were included in the deal. However, the sacrificial victims were not always enemies. There are tales of kings offering their sons to the gods in return for Odin's favour, and some stories seem to suggest even the king himself (or, more probably, a symbolic substitute for him) could be sacrificed in times of crisis or famine. One legend tells of a king drawing lots from the men of the kingdom to find a sacrificial victim, and choosing himself.

The practice of human sacrifice was not confined to men. The wives or women slaves of high-born warriors were thought to sacrifice themselves voluntarily on the burial fire when their men died. They would then be accorded honour and high esteem in the next world.

According to legend, the devotion of some warriors to their gods was such that they were prepared to go into battle without armour, so great was their confidence they would be protected. This may have given rise to the stories of the Berserks – the warriors of Odin, who trusted completely in him to spare them from death or even wounding. They would go into battle dressed in animal skins (usually a wolf or bear, most closely associated with the god). They howled like the animals as they ran to meet the enemy in a transcendent state, which must have put the fear of Odin into their opponents. Their fearlessness and ferocity attracted stories of their shape-shifting powers in battle.

The wearing of animal furs was also important in the divination ceremony known as the *seid*. This could be performed by either a man or a woman, but usually a *völva*, or wise woman, would take charge. Wearing a special costume and head-dress made of animal furs and carrying a staff, she called on the spirits before going into a trance and dispensing prophecies and advice. The ceremony is very similar to shamanistic rites in other primitive cultures.

Eating and Drinking   Food and drink played a very important part in Norse mythology, most famously in the feasting and carousing of the dead warriors in the halls of Valhalla (*see p. 175*). Drinking was central to legends of Odin's acquisition of knowledge, whether it be the mead of inspiration, or drinking from Mimir's spring (*see p. 169*). The wise giant Kvasir, created by the gods, was killed by dwarves who mixed his blood with honey to create the mead of inspiration; it gave the drinker the power to speak words of wisdom or compose fabulous verse. Odin retrieved the miraculous mixture and took it back to Asgard for the gods to use.

Norse Gods

The Norse gods were by no means infallible: all were subject to fate, the forces of nature (over which they had some, but not complete, control) and the cunning of others. In the end, they would all be destroyed in the overwhelming chaos of Ragnarok.

Given the huge cast of characters in Scandinavian legend, it can be hard to classify individuals – one name might refer to a god, a giant, a dwarf or a heroic mortal. Minor deities also confused the picture, and the same god might have different names in different areas. Even gods whose identities are clear had complex relationships, with inter-connected family networks and relationships with other worlds' beings .

The main gods fall into two groups – the Aesir and the Vanir. The gods of the Aesir were gods of the sky, war and justice, led by Odin and Thor; they were the beings worshipped by the aristocracy and warriors. The gods and goddesses of the lower classes were those of the Vanir, led by Freyr. The Vanir ruled the sea, and were protectors of the sources of life and food – as the gods of earth and fertility, they were favoured by farmers and hunters. Njord, father of Freyr, was said to be the god of sea and ships. Having two sets of gods with their own relationships and cults led to rivalry and confusion between devotees of the Aesir and the Vanir; rivalry which is reflected in stories of war between the two groups of gods.

Asgard was the realm of the Aesir, presided over by
Odin right at the top of Yggdrasil. It is depicted as
being like the better-known home of the Greek gods
on Mount Olympus – it is portrayed not as a perfect
paradise, but as a place of petty jealousy, squabbles
and mischief-making.

Aegir   The god of the ocean and the personification of
the sea, Aegir would rise out of the churning waters
with his great white beard, grasping ships to pull them
under the waves. Dead sailors were thought to feast
with Aegir and his wife Ran in much the same manner
as warriors in Valhalla caroused with Odin. Ran was
said to trap seafarers in her net and if they had gold,
they were guaranteed a good welcome. When danger
was imminent at sea, many sailors would hide a gold
coin around their person to ensure that they would
receive a good welcome in her halls. The nine
daughters of Aegir and Ran, the Wave Maidens, were
said to be the mothers of Heimdall (*see p. 185*).

Bragi   Aesir god of poetry and music; his wife was
Idun. Bragi was Odin's son, and his song, verse and
harp-playing welcomed dead warriors to Valhalla.

Forseti   God of law and justice, one of the Aesir gods.

Freya   The major Vanir goddess, she wore the enchanted Brisingamen necklace or girdle made by dwarves.
She was linked with the earth, childbirth and the

blessing of children, and the realm of the dead. Tales of Freya were similarities to those of the Aesir goddess Frigg, wife of Odin, and other goddesses of plenty from Celtic and Roman mythology. Freya married Od, of whom little is known other than that he shared some characteristics with Odin. But after he left her, she became notorious for a willingness to take many lovers.

Freyr Main god of the Vanir, his name means 'Lord'. Freya ('Lady') was his sister, and their father was the god Njord. Although they were Vanir gods, they lived in Asgard, where they had gone as hostages to the peace between the two sets of gods. Freyr dispensed peace and plenty, and he was invoked in marriage – sometimes being represented by a phallic image.

Frigga Wife of Odin, she was the mother of Balder and Hoder. She was the principle goddess of fertility.

Heimdall The White God and one of Asgard's most significant inhabitants after the great gods. He kept guard beside the rainbow bridge at the entrance to the fortress of the gods, by virtue of his exceptional sight and hearing. He carried a great horn to warn the gods when Ragnarok was at hand. His father was Odin and his mothers were the nine Wave Maidens.

Hel Ruler of the dead in the Norse underworld in Niflheim, she was the daughter of Loki. She is represented as the personification of death – half-black, half-white and terrible to look at. It is not known if she was meant to be alive or dead, and she may even have been a rotting corpse.

Hermod As messenger of the gods, Hermod welcomed the dead to Valhalla, and it was he who approached Hel to plead for the release of Balder (*see p. 173*).

Hlin A beautiful goddess who attended Frigga; she was the goddess of consolation, relieving grief and tears.

Hoder Also known as Hod, he was the twin brother and inadvertent slayer of Balder (*see p. 174*).

Idun Goddess of spring, she guarded the golden apples of eternal youth which prevented the gods from growing old.

Loki A very ambiguous character, Loki was the gods' chief trickster and mischief-maker. Half-wicked, half-helpful, he was a mixer who gloried in stirring trouble.

Loki is a very important character who regularly accompanies Thor and Odin and often seems to be helping and hindering them at the same time. Loki had a relationship with a hideous giantess which resulted in three grotesque offspring – the savage wolf Fenrir; the goddess of death, Hel; and the terrible World Serpent. The death of Balder (*see p. 173*) is due to Loki's malice – this story is also evidence of his ability to take both male and female forms. When the gods realised his part in Balder's killing, they trapped him under stones or bound him, Prometheus-like, in irons and set a poisonous snake to drip venom on his face; there he was destined to remain until Ragnarok.

Mimir Wisest of the gods, Mimir guarded the sacred spring of knowledge under the World Tree, known as Mimir's spring. Even when his head was cut off in the war between the Aesir and Vanir gods, it continued, disembodied, to guard the spring, and was consulted by Odin when he needed advice in times of crisis.

Nerthus A goddess reported by Tacitus to be worshipped around Denmark. Her name means 'Mother Earth', and she was the first wife of the god Njord, one of the main gods of the Vanir.

Njord The father of Freyr and Freya and was originally one of the gods of the Vanir; he was closely associated with the sea and ships. He went with his two children to live in Asgard as a hostage to secure the peace between Vanir and Aesir, and his dwelling place was Noatun ('Enclosure of ships'). He was thought to have power over the sea and the wind, granting good weather and favourable winds to those sailors and farmers who pleased him.

Odin Known as 'All-Father'; the other gods are sometimes referred to as the children of Odin. He also had many children across Midgard, which he roamed in disguise, seducing and impregnating mortal women.

A medieval depiction of Odin, here, being threatened by a monster

Odin was worshipped by warriors and leaders who occasionally received gifts from him: such was the great sword Gram, given to Sigmund the Volsung. Odin himself was said to have plunged the sword deep into the tree that formed the central pillar of the family hall and, with echoes of Arthur, only the young hero who won Odin's favour could draw it out.

Odin was a ferocious warrior, bordering on the mad– as were his battle followers, the Berserkers (*see p. 181*). Shifting and untrustworthy, he was also wise from his knowledge of the runes and the spirit-world. He was associated with death, especially in battle, where ravens, wolves and the Valkyries attended him. Also called Woden or Wodan, Wednesday is named for him.

Sif The wife of Thor. Her beautiful golden hair was cut off by Loki as she slept, which led Thor to demand recompense. Loki went to Svartalheim, the land of the dark elves, and asked them to make new hair for Sif as well as gifts for Odin and Freyr, in an attempt to win them over. The dwarves wove fine golden thread to replace Sif's hair, and created the spear Gungnir, which was given to Odin; the golden boar Gullinbursti for Freyr, and the great hammer, most powerful of all the gods' treasures, for Thor.

Thor As Odin's influence waned, the god of thunder became increasingly prominent and by the Viking era he was the most popular of all the gods. Red-bearded,

strong and powerful, lion-hearted and utterly faithful, able to eat and drink huge amounts and prone to fits of rage, he was the god all warriors wanted to be like. His great hammer, Mjollnir, was the most important of all the treasures of Asgard, protecting against giants and monsters. No matter how far he threw it, the enchanted hammer always returned like a boomerang to his hand – except the time it was stolen (*see p. 177*). Thor's cult was linked to the prosperity of the people and the well-being of the family, including fertility and the changing seasons. His marriage to Sif is a version of the ancient union of the sky god and earth goddess. Thursday is named after him.

Tyr The bravest of the warrior gods of the Aesir, he lost his hand fettering the ferocious wolf Fenrir. When the gods were attempting to bind the animal with enchanted cord, it refused to submit unless one of the gods put an arm its mouth as a guarantee that it was not a trap. Tyr volunteered and so lost his hand when the wolf realised it could not escape from its bonds.

Ull The god of winter, he was a fine archer, hunter and warrior. He is one of the less well-known gods.

Valkyries These warrior maidens of Odin were the choosers of the slain of battle, making their way through the field to select those who would die. They escorted the dead warriors to Valhalla, welcoming them with horns of mead and attending the banquet tables. The most famous Valkyrie was Brynhild. They may have had an association with particular families, as guardian spirits, befriending the warriors of each generation and welcoming them in death, in much the same way as the banshees of the Celtic tradition were associated with a particular clan.

INDEX OF THE GODS

Listings show each god's or spirit's main entry.

COLLINS GEM
BABIES'
names
a
?
z
a mine of information

COLLINS GEM
BEER
a mine of information

COLLINS GEM
BIRDS
a mine of information

COLLINS GEM
CALORIE
Counter
a mine of information

COLLINS GEM
FACT FILE
a mine of information

COLLINS GEM
FENG SHUI
a mine of information

COLLINS GEM
FLAGS
a mine of information

COLLINS GEM
Healthy
EATING
a mine of information

COLLINS GEM
QUOTATIONS
a mine of information

COLLINS GEM
SAS
Self-Defence
a mine of information

COLLINS GEM
SAS
Survival Guide
a mine of information

COLLINS GEM
SEASHORE
a mine of information

COLLINS GEM
TREES
a mine of information

COLLINS GEM
Understanding
DREAMS
a mine of information

COLLINS GEM
WILD
flowers
a mine of information

COLLINS GEM
WINE
Dictionary
a mine of information